CELPIP VOCABULARY PRACTICE

Ali Rastegari

VOCABULARY TOPICS

1. Health
2. Environment
3. Travel
4. Science
5. Technology
6. Education
7. Sports
8. Food and Nutrition
9. Business and Economics
10. Art and Culture
11. History
12. Politics and Government
13. Literature
14. Music
15. Fashion and Style
16. Philosophy and Ethics
17. Psychology
18. Religion and Spirituality
19. Social Issues
20. Prefixes and Suffixes
21. Film and Cinema
22. Geography
23. Law and Justice
24. Media and Communication
25. Economics

1. HEALTH

1. Wellness: Well-being, Healthiness
Definition: The state of being in good physical and mental health.
Example:
- She practices yoga and meditation to maintain her wellness.
- Regular exercise and a balanced diet contribute to overall well-being.
- The wellness program at work focuses on promoting a healthy lifestyle.
- Mental wellness involves taking care of one's emotional and psychological state.
- The spa offers various treatments for relaxation and enhancing wellness.

2. Epidemic: Outbreak, Plague
Definition: A widespread occurrence of a particular disease in a community or region.
Example:
- The city took swift action to contain the flu epidemic.
- The government declared a state of emergency due to the growing epidemic of malaria.
- The rapid spread of the virus led to a global epidemic.
- Health officials are monitoring the situation closely to prevent an epidemic.
- The epidemic has resulted in a significant increase in hospital admissions.

3. Vaccination: Immunization, Inoculation
Definition: The process of administering a vaccine to stimulate immunity against a specific disease.
Example:
- The doctor recommended getting a flu vaccination before

winter arrives.
- Childhood vaccinations have significantly reduced the incidence of certain diseases.
- Many countries have implemented nationwide vaccination campaigns to combat infectious diseases.
- It is important to follow the recommended vaccination schedule for maximum protection.
- The vaccination rate among school children has improved over the years.

4. Chronic: Persistent, Long-lasting

Definition: Persisting over a long period of time or recurring frequently.
Example:
- He suffers from chronic back pain, which affects his daily activities.
- Chronic stress can have detrimental effects on both physical and mental health.
- The patient's chronic condition requires ongoing medical management.
- The chronic nature of the disease necessitates regular check-ups and monitoring.
- Chronic illnesses often require lifestyle modifications and long-term treatment plans.

5. Diagnosis: Determination, Identification

Definition: The identification of a disease or condition through examination and analysis of symptoms.
Example:
- The doctor made a diagnosis of pneumonia based on the patient's chest x-ray.
- It took several medical tests to reach a conclusive diagnosis.
- Early diagnosis of cancer greatly improves the chances of successful treatment.
- The accurate diagnosis of the illness allowed for appropriate medical intervention.

- The diagnosis confirmed the presence of a bacterial infection.

6. Symptom: Indication, Manifestation
Definition: A physical or mental indication of a disease or disorder experienced by a person.
Example:
- Fever is a common symptom of the flu.
- Fatigue and loss of appetite are typical symptoms of depression.
- One of the symptoms of allergies is sneezing and itchy eyes.
- The doctor asked about other accompanying symptoms to make a more accurate diagnosis.
- The patient described the symptoms she was experiencing in detail to the healthcare provider.

7. Prevention: Avoidance, Prophylaxis
Definition: Actions taken to avoid or minimize the occurrence of a disease or health problem.
- Regular exercise and a balanced diet are key to the prevention of heart disease.
- Vaccinations play a crucial role in the prevention of infectious diseases.
- The government launched a public awareness campaign to promote the prevention of smoking.
- Early detection and screening can aid in the prevention of certain types of cancer.
- The promotion of hand hygiene is a simple yet effective measure for disease prevention.

8. Rehabilitation: Therapy, Recovery
Definition: The process of restoring someone's physical or mental health through therapy and treatment.
Example:
- After the surgery, he underwent rehabilitation to regain strength and mobility.
- The rehabilitation center offers various programs for individuals recovering from substance abuse.

- Physical rehabilitation after a sports injury is essential for a full recovery.
- The stroke patient made significant progress through intensive rehabilitation.
- The team of healthcare professionals collaborated to develop a personalized rehabilitation plan.

9. Medication: Medicine, Drug
Definition: A substance used to cure, or alleviate the symptoms of a disease.
Example:
- She takes medication daily to control her blood pressure.
- The doctor prescribed a new medication to relieve her chronic migraines.
- It's important to follow the prescribed dosage and frequency when taking medication.
- The pharmacy stocks a wide range of medications for various health conditions.
- The side effects of the medication were carefully explained by the pharmacist.

10. Immunity: Resistance, Protection
Definition: The ability of an organism to resist or defend against a specific disease or foreign substance.
- After recovering from COVID-19, he developed immunity to the virus.
- Vaccinations help build immunity against infectious diseases.
- The immune system plays a crucial role in protecting the body from pathogens.
- Malnutrition can weaken the immune system, making individuals more susceptible to infections.
- The presence of antibodies indicates a level of immunity to a particular disease.

11. Therapy: Rehabilitation, Treatment
Definition: The treatment of a disease or disorder through medical or psychological means.

Example:
- She attends regular physical therapy sessions to improve her mobility after the accident.
- Cognitive-behavioral therapy is often used to treat anxiety disorders.
- The therapist provided individualized therapy to address the patient's specific needs.
- Music therapy has been shown to have positive effects on mental well-being.
- The child with speech difficulties benefited greatly from speech therapy.

12. Pandemic: Global outbreak, Worldwide epidemic

Definition: An outbreak of a disease that occurs over a wide geographic area and affects an exceptionally high proportion of the population.
Example:
- The COVID-19 pandemic has had a significant impact on global health and economies.
- The World Health Organization declared the outbreak a pandemic.
- The government implemented strict measures to control the spread of the pandemic.
- The healthcare system faced immense challenges during the peak of the pandemic.
- The pandemic highlighted the importance of public health preparedness.

13. Contagious: Infectious, Transmissible

Definition: Capable of being transmitted or spread to others, typically through direct or indirect contact.
Example:
- Measles is highly contagious and can spread quickly among unvaccinated individuals.
- The doctor advised the patient to stay home as the illness was highly contagious.

- Hand hygiene is crucial in preventing the spread of contagious diseases.
- The contagious nature of the virus necessitated strict quarantine measures.
- The school temporarily closed due to an outbreak of a contagious illness.

14. Rehabilitation: Therapy, Recovery
Definition: The process of restoring someone's physical or mental health through therapy and treatment.
Example:
- After the surgery, he underwent rehabilitation to regain strength and mobility.
- The rehabilitation center offers various programs for individuals recovering from substance abuse.
- Physical rehabilitation after a sports injury is essential for a full recovery.
- The stroke patient made significant progress through intensive rehabilitation.

15. Diagnosis: Determination, Identification
Definition: The identification of disease through examination and analysis of symptoms.
Example:
- The doctor made a diagnosis of pneumonia based on the patient's chest x-ray.
- It took several medical tests to reach a conclusive diagnosis.
- Early diagnosis of cancer greatly improves the chances of successful treatment.
- The accurate diagnosis of the illness allowed for appropriate medical intervention.
- The diagnosis confirmed the presence of a bacterial infection.

16. Symptom: Indication, Manifestation
Definition: A physical or mental indication of a disease or disorder experienced by a person.
Example:

- Fever is a common symptom of the flu.
- Fatigue and loss of appetite are typical symptoms of depression.
- One of the symptoms of allergies is sneezing and itchy eyes.
- The doctor asked about other accompanying symptoms to make a more accurate diagnosis.
- The patient described the symptoms she was experiencing in detail to the healthcare provider.

17. Prevention: Avoidance, Prophylaxis
Definition: Actions taken to avoid or minimize the occurrence of a disease or health problem.
Example:
- Regular exercise and a balanced diet are key to the prevention of heart disease.
- Vaccinations play a crucial role in the prevention of infectious diseases.
- The government launched a public awareness campaign to promote the prevention of smoking.
- Early detection and screening can aid in the prevention of certain types of cancer.
- The promotion of hand hygiene is a simple yet effective measure for disease prevention.

18. Medication: Medicine, Drug
Definition: A substance used to treat, cure, or alleviate the symptoms of a disease or medical condition.
Example:
- She takes medication daily to control her blood pressure.
- The doctor prescribed a new medication to relieve her chronic migraines.
- It's important to follow the prescribed dosage and frequency when taking medication.
- The pharmacy stocks a wide range of medications for various health conditions.
- The side effects of the medication were carefully explained by

the pharmacist.

19. Immunity: Resistance, Protection
Definition: The ability of an organism to resist or defend against a specific disease or foreign substance.
Example:
- After recovering from COVID-19, he developed immunity to the virus.
- Vaccinations help build immunity against infectious diseases.
- The immune system plays a crucial role in protecting the body from pathogens.
- Malnutrition can weaken the immune system, making individuals more susceptible to infections.
- The presence of antibodies indicates a level of immunity to a particular disease.

20. Therapy: Rehabilitation, Treatment
Definition: The treatment of a disease or disorder through medical or psychological means.
Example:
- She attends regular physical therapy sessions to improve her mobility after the accident.
- Cognitive-behavioral therapy is often used to treat anxiety disorders.
- The therapist provided individualized therapy to address the patient's specific needs.
- Music therapy has been shown to have positive effects on mental well-being.
- The child with speech difficulties benefited greatly from speech therapy.

2. ENVIRONMENT

1. Sustainability: Environmental responsibility, Conservation
Definition: The practice of using resources in a way that preserves the environment for future generations.
Example:
- The company is committed to sustainability and has implemented eco-friendly initiatives.
- Renewable energy sources such as solar and wind power contribute to sustainability.
- Recycling is an essential part of sustainable waste management.
- The government has set targets to reduce carbon emissions and promote sustainability.
- Sustainable agriculture practices aim to minimize environmental impact while ensuring food production.

2. Biodiversity: Ecological diversity, Species variety
Definition: The variety of plant and animal species in a particular habitat or on Earth as a whole.
Example:
- Rainforests are known for their high levels of biodiversity.
- The loss of habitats has resulted in a significant decline in biodiversity.
- Conservation efforts focus on protecting and preserving biodiversity.
- The study aims to assess the impact of climate change on marine biodiversity.
- Biodiversity is essential for maintaining the balance of ecosystems.

3. Conservation: Preservation, Protection
Definition: The act of protecting and preserving natural resources and the environment.

Example:
- National parks are established for the conservation of wildlife and natural beauty.
- Conservation programs aim to restore and protect endangered species.
- Water conservation is important in regions facing drought conditions.
- The organization works tirelessly for the conservation of marine habitats.
- The community actively participates in recycling initiatives for waste conservation.

4. Pollution: Contamination, Environmental degradation
Definition: The presence of harmful substances or pollutants in the environment, resulting in adverse effects on living organisms.
Example:
- Air pollution from vehicle emissions poses a significant health risk in urban areas.
- Efforts to reduce plastic pollution have gained momentum worldwide.
- Water pollution from industrial waste affects aquatic life and ecosystems.
- The government has implemented stricter regulations to control pollution from factories.
- The cleanup of oil spills is crucial to prevent environmental pollution.

5. Climate change: global warming, climate crisis
Definition: Long-term shifts in temperature patterns and weather conditions on earth, primarily caused by human activities.
Example:
- The scientific consensus is that human activities contribute to climate change.
- Rising sea levels are one of the consequences of climate change.

- The need to reduce greenhouse gas emissions is critical to combat climate change.
- Climate change poses challenges for agricultural production and food security.
- The international community is working together to address the impacts of climate change.

6. Deforestation: Forest depletion, Clear-cutting
Definition: The clearing or removal of forests, primarily for human activities such as agriculture, logging, or urbanization.
Example:
- Deforestation in the Amazon rainforest threatens biodiversity and contributes to climate change.
- Efforts are being made to combat deforestation through sustainable forestry practices.
- The government implemented strict regulations to curb illegal deforestation.
- Deforestation has led to the displacement of indigenous communities and the loss of traditional lands.
- Reforestation initiatives aim to restore areas affected by deforestation.

7. Anthropogenic: Human-induced, Man-made
Definition: Caused or influenced by human activity.
Example:
- The increase in carbon dioxide levels in the atmosphere is primarily due to anthropogenic emissions from burning fossil fuels.
- Deforestation is an anthropogenic factor that contributes to the loss of biodiversity.
- The construction of highways has resulted in the fragmentation of natural habitats, leading to anthropogenic disturbances.
- Governments worldwide are implementing measures to reduce anthropogenic greenhouse gas emissions.
- The impact of anthropogenic pollution on marine ecosystems

is a growing concern.

8. Ecosystem: Habitat, Biome
Definition: A community of living organisms and their interactions with each other and their environment.
Example:
- Coral reefs are highly diverse and fragile ecosystems.
- The destruction of wetland ecosystems has negative impacts on water quality.
- Conservation efforts aim to preserve and restore natural ecosystems.
- Human activities can disrupt the balance of ecosystems, leading to biodiversity loss.
- The protection of keystone species is crucial for maintaining ecosystem stability.

9. Resilience: Adaptability, Endurance
Definition: The ability of an ecosystem to recover and adapt to disturbances or changes.

Example:
- Wetland ecosystems exhibit a remarkable resilience to flooding, thanks to their natural water storage capacity.
- The coral reef's resilience allows it to recover from bleaching events over time.
- Conservation strategies focus on enhancing the resilience of ecosystems in the face of climate change.
- The resilience of a forest ecosystem can be assessed by its ability to regenerate after a wildfire.
- Climate-resilient agriculture practices aim to enhance food production while adapting to changing climatic conditions.

10. Greenhouse effect: Global warming effect, Climate change effect
Definition: The trapping of heat in the Earth's atmosphere by certain gases, such as carbon dioxide, causing an increase in

global temperatures.
Example:
- The greenhouse effect is a natural phenomenon that helps regulate the Earth's temperature.
- Increased greenhouse gas emissions from human activities have intensified the greenhouse effect.
- The consequences of the greenhouse effect include rising sea levels and changes in weather patterns.
- Mitigating the greenhouse effect requires reducing carbon emissions and adopting sustainable practices.
- Scientists study the greenhouse effect to better understand its impacts on the environment.

11. Conservationist: Environmentalist, Naturalist
Definition: A person who advocates for the protection and preservation of natural resources and the environment.
Example:
- The conservationist has dedicated his life to preserving endangered species.
- Conservationists work to raise awareness about the importance of sustainable practices.
- The organization collaborates with local communities and conservationists to protect wildlife habitats.
- The renowned conservationist has made significant contributions to environmental research.
- The conservationist is actively involved in lobbying for stricter environmental regulations.

12. Carbon footprint: Environmental footprint, Carbon emissions
Definition: The total amount of greenhouse gases, primarily carbon dioxide, emitted by an individual, organization, or activity.
Example:
- Individuals can reduce their carbon footprint by using public transportation or cycling instead of driving.

- Companies are increasingly adopting sustainable practices to lower their carbon footprint.
- The carbon footprint of the manufacturing industry contributes to climate change.
- Carbon offset programs help individuals and businesses offset their carbon emissions.
- Calculating and reducing carbon footprints are important steps toward environmental sustainability.

13. Degradation: Deterioration, Decline
Definition: The process of deteriorating or damaging something, often referring to the decline of environmental quality or the destruction of habitats.
Example:
- Deforestation and pollution lead to the degradation of natural landscapes and the loss of biodiversity.
- Soil degradation resulting from intensive agriculture can have long-term negative effects on crop productivity.
- The degradation of coral reefs is a pressing environmental issue that threatens marine ecosystems.
- Urbanization often contributes to the degradation of air and water quality in cities.
- Efforts to combat land degradation include implementing erosion control measures and sustainable land management practices.

14. Ecological footprint: Environmental footprint, Sustainability footprint
Definition: The measure of human impact on the environment in terms of land, water, resources consumed, and waste generated.
Example:
- The ecological footprint is a tool used to assess and track the sustainability of human activities.
- Individuals can reduce their ecological footprint by adopting energy-efficient practices and reducing waste.

- The ecological footprint of industrialized nations is significantly higher compared to developing countries.
- Sustainable development aims to minimize the ecological footprint while meeting human needs.
- Governments and organizations use ecological footprint analysis to inform policy and decision-making.

15. Wildlife conservation: Animal preservation, Biodiversity protection

Definition: The efforts to protect and preserve endangered species and their habitats.

Example:
- National parks play a crucial role in wildlife conservation.
- The organization focuses on wildlife conservation through habitat restoration projects.
- The illegal wildlife trade poses a significant threat to global conservation efforts.
- Conservationists work tirelessly to combat poaching and protect vulnerable wildlife.
- The success of wildlife conservation relies on public support and education.

16. Environmental impact: Ecological footprint, Environmental influence

Definition: The effect of human activities on the environment, including the depletion of resources, pollution, and habitat destruction.

Example:
- Large-scale agriculture has a significant environmental impact due to pesticide use and deforestation.
- Environmental impact assessments are conducted before major construction projects.
- The shift toward renewable energy sources aims to minimize the environmental impact of energy production.
- Consumer choices can have a direct impact on the environment, such as reducing single-use plastics.

- Sustainable practices in industries are essential for reducing their environmental impact.

17. Greenwashing: Environmental deception, Eco-fraud
Definition: The practice of misleading consumers into believing that a company or product is more environmentally friendly than it actually is.
Example:
- Some companies engage in greenwashing by making false or exaggerated claims about their environmental practices.
- Consumers should be cautious and do their research to identify genuine environmentally friendly products from greenwashing.
- The rise of greenwashing has led to the need for stricter regulations and transparent labeling practices.
- Environmental organizations play a role in exposing greenwashing and holding companies accountable.
- Educating consumers about greenwashing helps promote informed and responsible purchasing decisions.

18. Stewardship: Custodianship, Responsibility
Definition: The responsible management and care of something entrusted to one's protection.
Example:
- Environmental stewardship requires individuals and organizations to adopt sustainable practices and conserve natural resources.
- The indigenous community has a deep sense of stewardship for the land and its natural resources.
- Corporate stewardship involves integrating environmental and social considerations into business operations.
- The government has a role in promoting stewardship through policy frameworks and regulations.
- Effective environmental stewardship requires collaboration between various stakeholders.

19. Habitat: Environment, Ecosystem
Definition: The natural environment in which a particular

species or organism lives and depends on for survival.
Example:
- Wetlands serve as vital habitats for various species of birds and aquatic life.
- Destruction of natural habitats threatens the survival of many endangered species.
- Conservation efforts aim to protect and restore critical habitats for wildlife.
- The loss of habitat due to deforestation has led to the decline of certain animal species.
- Preserving and maintaining diverse habitats is essential for supporting biodiversity.

20. Ecotourism: Sustainable tourism, Responsible travel

Definition: Tourism that promotes the conservation of natural environments, supports local communities, and educates visitors about ecological and cultural values.
Example:
- Ecotourism provides opportunities for travellers to experience and appreciate the natural beauty of an area without causing harm.
- Responsible travellers choose ecotourism activities that have a positive impact on the environment and local communities.
- Ecotourism can contribute to the preservation of endangered habitats and wildlife.
- The ecotourism industry plays a crucial role in raising awareness and funds for conservation efforts.
- Local communities benefit economically from ecotourism by providing services and sharing their cultural heritage.

3. TRAVEL

1. Expedition: Journey, Exploration
Definition: A journey or voyage undertaken for a specific purpose, often involving exploration or research.
Example:
- The scientific expedition aimed to study the biodiversity of the rainforest.
- They embarked on an arduous expedition to reach the summit of the mountain.
- The archaeological expedition uncovered ancient artifacts in the remote desert.
- The team organized an expedition to document the effects of climate change in the Arctic.
- The adventurers set off on an expedition to cross the treacherous jungle.

2. Itinerary: Travel plan, Schedule
Definition: A detailed plan or schedule of a journey, including the places to be visited and the dates and times of travel.
Example:
- The travel agency provided a well-organized itinerary for their trip to Europe.
- They followed their carefully planned itinerary to visit the famous landmarks in the city.
- The itinerary included guided tours, museum visits, and free exploration time.
- She modified her itinerary to accommodate an additional day in the coastal town.
- The detailed itinerary helped them stay on track and make the most of their limited time.

3. Accommodation: Lodging, Housing
Definition: A place where travellers can stay overnight or for a

period of time.
Example:
- They booked a comfortable accommodation in a boutique hotel near the city center.
- The tourist town offers a variety of accommodation options, including hotels, guesthouses, and vacation rentals.
- The camping site provides affordable accommodation for outdoor enthusiasts.
- The hostel offers budget-friendly accommodation for backpackers and solo travellers.
- They were satisfied with the quality of their accommodation and the friendly staff.

4. Souvenir: Memento, Keepsake
Definition: An item or object kept as a reminder or token of a place visited or an experience gained while travelling.
Example:
- She purchased a traditional keychain as a souvenir from her trip to Japan.
- The local market is filled with souvenirs such as handmade crafts and artwork.
- The photo album serves as a cherished souvenir of their family vacation.
- He brought back souvenirs for his friends, including postcards and local delicacies.
- The souvenir shop offers a wide range of products, from T-shirts to fridge magnets.

5. Backpacking: Independent travel, Budget travel
Definition: Traveling with only a backpack, often on a low budget and with a focus on experiencing new cultures and adventures.
Example:
- They decided to go backpacking through Southeast Asia during their summer break.
- Backpacking allows you to immerse yourself in the local

culture and meet fellow travellers.
- The backpacking trip included staying in hostels and cooking meals in shared kitchens.
- She documented her backpacking adventures through a blog and social media.
- The backpacking community provides valuable tips and advice for budget travellers.

6. Tourist attraction: Sightseeing spot, Landmark

Definition: A place or site that is popular and interesting to tourists, often due to its historical, cultural, or natural significance.
Example:
- The ancient ruins are a major tourist attraction, drawing visitors from around the world.
- The city's famous cathedral is a must-visit tourist attraction.
- The tourist attraction offers guided tours to learn about its rich history.
- The national park is known for its stunning landscapes and unique wildlife, making it a popular tourist attraction.
- The tourist attraction provides breathtaking views of the city skyline.

7. Cultural heritage: Heritage, Tradition

Definition: The customs, traditions, artifacts, and values that are passed down through generations and contribute to the identity of a particular society or community.
Example:
- The preservation of cultural heritage is essential for maintaining a sense of identity and history.
- The museum showcases the cultural heritage of the region through its collection of art and artifacts.
- The UNESCO designation recognizes the importance of preserving and protecting cultural heritage sites.
- The local community takes pride in their cultural heritage and celebrates it through festivals and events.

- The government implements policies to safeguard cultural heritage from destruction and illegal trade.

8. Local cuisine: Traditional food, Regional dishes
Definition: The traditional or characteristic food and cooking practices of a specific region or country.
Example:
- One of the highlights of travelling is trying the local cuisine and experiencing new flavours.
- The street food stalls offer a variety of local cuisine, from spicy noodles to savoury snacks.
- The cooking class provides an opportunity to learn how to prepare authentic local cuisine.
- The restaurant specializes in serving traditional dishes that showcase the flavours of the local cuisine.
- Exploring the local markets allows you to taste and purchase ingredients used in the regional cuisine.

9. Ecotourism: Sustainable tourism, Nature tourism
Definition: Responsible travel to natural areas that conserves the environment, sustains the well-being of the local community, and involves education and interpretation.
- The national park attracts visitors interested in ecotourism and wildlife conservation.
- The eco-lodge promotes ecotourism by offering sustainable accommodation and nature-based activities.
- The tour guide provided information about the local ecosystem and the principles of ecotourism.
- Ecotourism initiatives aim to support local communities and preserve natural habitats.
- The travellers chose an ecotourism operator that prioritizes minimizing the negative impacts on the environment.

10. Cultural exchange: Cross-cultural interaction, Cultural interchange
Definition: The interaction and sharing of ideas, customs, traditions, and experiences between people from different

cultural backgrounds.
Example:
- The study abroad program fosters cultural exchange by immersing students in a foreign country.
- The international festival promotes cultural exchange through music, dance, and food from various cultures.
- The exchange program allowed students to live with host families and experience the local culture firsthand.
- The language exchange program provides an opportunity for cultural exchange while practicing language skills.
- The organization facilitates cultural exchange programs to enhance mutual understanding and appreciation.

11. Hospitality: Warmth, Welcome
Definition: The friendly and generous reception and treatment of guests or strangers.
Example:
- The hotel staff's hospitality made the guests feel welcomed and comfortable.
- The locals' hospitality extended beyond offering directions, as they invited the visitors into their homes.
- The region is known for its hospitality, with locals often going out of their way to assist travellers.
- The hospitality industry plays a significant role in the economic development of tourist destinations.
- The hospitality training program focuses on customer service skills and cultural sensitivity.

12. Landmark: Icon, Monument
Definition: An easily recognizable feature or structure that is considered a symbol or significant representation of a place or historical period.
Example:
- The Eiffel Tower is an iconic landmark of Paris and a popular tourist attraction.
- The ancient ruins are a significant landmark that showcases

the city's rich history.
- The Statue of Liberty is a well-known landmark in New York City, representing freedom and democracy.
- The archaeological site contains ancient landmarks that offer insights into past civilizations.
- The city's skyline is dotted with architectural landmarks that reflect its modernity and progress.

13. Adventure: Excursion, Thrill

Definition: An exciting and unusual experience or activity that involves risk, often in a natural or remote setting.
Example:
- They embarked on an adventure tour, which included activities such as hiking and white-water rafting.
- The adventurers sought thrilling adventures, such as skydiving and bungee jumping.
- The national park offers various adventure activities, including rock climbing and zip-lining.
- The travel agency specializes in organizing adventure trips for adrenaline enthusiasts.
- Exploring the uncharted wilderness provided a sense of adventure and discovery.

14. Duty-free: Tax-free, Exempt from duty

Definition: Referring to goods that can be purchased without paying certain taxes or duties, typically available in airports or specific shopping areas.
Example:
- They bought perfume and chocolates at the duty-free shop before boarding the plane.
- Duty-free shopping allows travellers to save money on luxury items and souvenirs.
- The duty-free section offers a wide selection of alcohol, tobacco, and cosmetics.
- Certain countries have duty-free allowances that specify the quantity and value of goods that can be brought in without

paying taxes.
- Travelers can enjoy tax-free shopping in designated duty-free zones.

15. Tour guide: Tour leader, Travel guide
Definition: A person who provides information, guidance, and commentary on the historical, cultural, and natural aspects of a place or attraction during a tour.
Example:
- The knowledgeable tour guide shared interesting facts about the historical landmarks.
- The tour guide led the group through the museum, providing insights into the artwork.
- The experienced tour guide took them on a walking tour, highlighting the city's architecture.
- The tour package includes the services of a professional tour guide throughout the itinerary.
- The tour guide's storytelling skills added depth and context to the sightseeing experience.

16. Jet lag: Time zone syndrome, Circadian rhythm disruption
Definition: A temporary condition experienced by travellers when crossing multiple time zones, resulting in fatigue, sleep disturbances, and disorientation.
Example:
- They experienced jet lag after a long-haul flight, struggling to adjust to the new time zone.
- To minimize jet lag, it is recommended to stay hydrated and adjust sleeping patterns gradually.
- The symptoms of jet lag include fatigue, insomnia, and difficulty concentrating.
- The traveller allowed themselves a day to rest and recover from jet lag before starting their sightseeing.
- Jet lag can affect travellers differently, and it may take a few days to fully adjust to the new time zone.

17. Currency exchange: Foreign exchange, Money conversion
Definition: The process of converting one currency into another, usually for the purpose of facilitating financial transactions in a foreign country.
Example:
- They exchanged their local currency for euros at the airport's currency exchange counter.
- The bank offers competitive rates for currency exchange, allowing travellers to get the best value for their money.
- The traveller used a currency exchange app to check the current exchange rates before making a transaction.
- It is convenient to have some local currency on hand for small expenses upon arrival, so they visited a currency exchange booth.
- The currency exchange service charges a small commission fee for converting currencies.

18. Layover: Stopover, Transit
Definition: A period of time during a journey when a traveller has to wait at an intermediate location before continuing their trip.
Example:
- Their flight had a six-hour layover in Dubai, giving them time to explore the city.
- The layover allowed them to visit a nearby attraction and experience a taste of the local culture.
- During the layover, passengers can relax in the airport lounge or take a nap in designated rest areas.
- The layover was extended due to a flight delay, requiring passengers to adjust their travel plans.
- They made the most of their layover by taking a guided tour of the city's landmarks.

19. Baggage claim: Luggage retrieval, Baggage reclaim
Definition: The area in an airport where passengers collect their checked-in luggage or bags after arriving at their destination.

Example:
- They proceeded to the baggage claim area to retrieve their suitcases.
- Baggage claim signs direct passengers to the designated conveyor belts for their flights.
- It is important to check the baggage claim tags to ensure you collect the correct luggage.
- The traveler reported a missing bag at the baggage claim counter and filed a claim.
- Heavy traffic in the baggage claim area caused a delay in retrieving their suitcases.

20. Customs: Border control, Immigration

Definition: The official process and procedures implemented by a country to regulate the movement of goods and people across its borders.

Example:
- All passengers must go through customs upon arrival to declare any goods or items subject to customs regulations.
- Customs officers conduct inspections to prevent the smuggling of illegal substances or prohibited items.
- The traveller completed the customs declaration form before passing through customs control.
- It is important to be aware of the customs regulations of the destination country to avoid any legal issues.
- The customs clearance process can vary in duration, depending on the volume of passengers and goods.

4. Science

1. Hypothesis: Theory, Assumption
Definition: A proposed explanation or prediction based on limited evidence, used as a starting point for scientific investigation.

Example:
- The scientist formulated a hypothesis to explain the observed phenomenon.
- The hypothesis suggests that increased exposure to sunlight leads to vitamin D production in the body.
- The researchers conducted experiments to test their hypothesis about the effects of caffeine on memory.
- The hypothesis was supported by the data collected during the study.
- Further research is needed to confirm or refute the initial hypothesis.

2. Experiment: Test, Trial
Definition: A controlled procedure carried out to gather data, validate hypotheses, or demonstrate a scientific principle.

Example:
- The scientists designed an experiment to investigate the effects of temperature on plant growth.
- In the experiment, two groups of mice were subjected to different conditions to compare their behavior.
- The results of the experiment indicated a strong correlation between exercise and cognitive function.
- The experiment was repeated multiple times to ensure the reliability of the findings.
- The students conducted a simple experiment to observe the chemical reaction.

3. Variable: Factor, Element

Definition: A measurable or controllable quantity that can vary or have different values in an experiment or study.
Example:
- The researchers identified several variables that could potentially influence the outcome of the study.
- Temperature was a critical variable in the experiment, affecting the rate of enzyme activity.
- The scientists manipulated the independent variable to observe its effect on the dependent variable.
- Controlling for confounding variables is important to isolate the impact of the variable of interest.
- The study analyzed the relationship between socioeconomic status and various health variables.

4. Data: Information, Facts
Definition: Facts, statistics, or information collected and analyzed as a basis for reasoning, discussion, or calculation.
Example:
- The experiment generated a large amount of data that needed to be analyzed.
- The researchers presented their findings based on the data collected from the survey.
- The data showed a clear correlation between smoking and lung cancer incidence.
- The study collected demographic data to understand population trends and patterns.
- Data from previous studies were used to support the conclusions drawn in the research.

5. Analysis: Examination, Study
Definition: The process of examining data, information, or a problem to uncover patterns, relationships, or insights.
Example:
- The analysis of the DNA samples revealed a genetic mutation associated with the disease.
- The researchers used statistical analysis to interpret the results

of the experiment.
- The analysis of the climate data indicated a significant increase in global temperatures.
- The study involved a detailed analysis of the impact of pollution on marine ecosystems.
- The data analysis supported the hypothesis that there is a link between stress and cardiovascular health.

6. Conclusion: Findings, Result
Definition: A judgment or decision reached after considering the evidence, data, or analysis of a study or experiment.
Example:
- Based on the results, the researchers drew the conclusion that the drug is effective in treating the disease.
- The study's conclusion suggested that regular exercise has a positive impact on mental well-being.
- The conclusion of the experiment supported the hypothesis proposed at the beginning.
- The researchers emphasized the limitations of the study in the final conclusion.
- In conclusion, the data showed a clear correlation between sleep duration and cognitive performance.

7. Theory: Principle, Concept
Definition: A well-substantiated explanation of some aspect of the natural world, supported by evidence and repeated testing.
Example:
- The theory of relativity revolutionized our understanding of space, time, and gravity.
- The scientists proposed a new theory to explain the observed phenomenon.
- The theory of evolution is supported by a vast body of evidence from various scientific disciplines.
- The theory predicts that increasing the temperature will accelerate the rate of chemical reactions.
- The study provided empirical support for the theory of

cognitive development.

8. Law: Rule, Principle

Definition: A statement that describes an observed pattern or phenomenon in nature, usually expressed as a mathematical equation.

Example:

- The law of gravity explains the attraction between objects with mass.
- According to the first law of thermodynamics, energy cannot be created or destroyed, only converted.
- The researchers discovered a new law governing the behavior of particles in quantum physics.
- The law of conservation of mass states that matter cannot be created or destroyed in a chemical reaction.
- The study confirmed the validity of Boyle's law, which relates the pressure and volume of a gas.

9. Experimentation: Testing, Trial

Definition: The act or process of carrying out experiments or tests to gather data or investigate a hypothesis.

- Scientific progress often relies on rigorous experimentation and systematic observation.
- The researcher proposed a new method of experimentation to overcome the limitations of previous studies.
- Ethical considerations should be taken into account when designing experiments involving human subjects.
- The field of medicine benefits from constant experimentation and the development of new treatments.
- The scientists conducted a series of controlled experiments to study the effects of the drug.

10. Observation: Perception, Monitoring

Definition: The act or process of noticing or perceiving something through careful watching or examination.

Example:

- The study involved direct observation of animal behaviour in

their natural habitat.
- The scientists made detailed observations of the celestial bodies using powerful telescopes.
- The participant's behaviour was recorded and analyzed based on careful observation during the experiment.
- The researchers noted an interesting observation regarding the relationship between temperature and plant growth.
- The study relied on qualitative observations to gain insights into human interaction patterns.

11. Peer review: Evaluation, Assessment
Definition: The process in which experts in a field assess the quality, validity, and originality of research before publication.
Example:
- The research paper underwent a rigorous peer review process before being accepted for publication.
- Peer review ensures that scientific studies meet the highest standards of quality and accuracy.
- The findings of the study were critically evaluated through the peer review process.
- The researcher received valuable feedback from peers during the peer review stage.
- The journal has a reputation for publishing articles that have undergone rigorous peer review.

12. Scientific method: Research process, Inquiry
Definition: A systematic approach to scientific investigation that involves observation, hypothesis formulation, experimentation, and analysis.
- The scientific method provides a structured framework for conducting research and gaining knowledge.
- The student followed the steps of the scientific method to investigate a chemical reaction.
- The researcher designed an experiment based on the principles of the scientific method.
- The scientific method allows scientists to draw reliable

conclusions from empirical evidence.
- Understanding the scientific method is crucial for conducting valid and reliable research.

13. Biotechnology: Genetic engineering, Bioengineering

Definition: The use of living organisms, biological systems, or their components to develop or create products and processes.
Example:
- Biotechnology has led to advancements in medicine, agriculture, and environmental protection.
- The researchers applied biotechnology techniques to develop a more efficient method of crop production.
- Genetic modification is a prominent aspect of biotechnology that allows for the manipulation of DNA.
- The biotechnology industry plays a significant role in the development of new pharmaceuticals.
- The study explored the ethical implications of biotechnology in the field of genetic engineering.

14. Genetic diversity: Variability, Genetic variation

Definition: The variety and differences in the genetic makeup of individuals within a species or population.
Example:
- Genetic diversity is essential for the long-term survival and adaptation of species to changing environments.
- The study examined the genetic diversity of a rare plant species to assess its conservation status.
- Loss of habitat can lead to a reduction in genetic diversity within animal populations.
- Genetic diversity is a key factor in the resilience and resistance of ecosystems to environmental changes.
- Conservation efforts aim to protect and preserve genetic diversity in endangered species.

15. Climate change: Global warming, Climate crisis

Definition: Long-term shifts or alterations in temperature patterns, weather conditions, and atmospheric conditions on a global scale.

Example:

- Climate change is primarily driven by human activities, including the burning of fossil fuels.
- The study investigated the effects of climate change on biodiversity in coastal regions.
- Rising sea levels and extreme weather events are among the consequences of climate change.
- The international community is working together to mitigate the impacts of climate change.
- The researchers developed models to predict future climate change scenarios.

16. Sustainable development: Eco-friendly development, Responsible growth

Definition: Development that meets the needs of the present generation without compromising the ability of future generations to meet their own needs.

Example:

- Sustainable development aims to strike a balance between economic growth, social equity, and environmental protection.
- The study assessed the sustainability of various agricultural practices in terms of their environmental impact.
- Governments worldwide are implementing policies to promote sustainable development and reduce carbon emissions.
- The company adopted sustainable practices, such as using renewable energy sources and reducing waste.
- Sustainable development requires the collective efforts of individuals, organizations, and governments.

17. Genetic mutation: Gene mutation, Genetic alteration

Definition: A permanent change in the DNA sequence of a gene or chromosome, resulting in a genetic variant.

Example:

- The study identified a specific genetic mutation associated with a rare genetic disorder.

- Genetic mutations can either be inherited or occur spontaneously during DNA replication.
- Researchers are investigating the potential implications of a newly discovered genetic mutation.
- Mutations in the BRCA genes are linked to an increased risk of developing breast and ovarian cancer.
- Understanding the mechanism behind genetic mutations is crucial in advancing genetic research.

18. Genetic engineering: Genetic modification, Genetic manipulation

Definition: The manipulation of an organism's genetic material to introduce new traits or modify existing ones.

Example:
- Genetic engineering has revolutionized medicine by enabling the production of life-saving drugs.
- The study focused on the ethical implications of genetic engineering in the field of human enhancement.
- Genetically engineered crops have the potential to improve agricultural productivity and reduce the use of pesticides.
- The researchers used genetic engineering techniques to enhance the nutritional content of a crop.
- Public debates surround the safety and long-term effects of genetic engineering in food production.

19. Biodiversity: Biological diversity, Variety of life

Definition: The variety and variability of living organisms, including plants, animals, and microorganisms, within a given ecosystem or on Earth as a whole.

Example:
- Biodiversity is crucial for maintaining ecosystem stability and resilience in the face of environmental changes.
- The loss of biodiversity poses a significant threat to global ecosystems and the services they provide.
- The study assessed the impact of deforestation on biodiversity in the Amazon rainforest.

- Conservation efforts focus on preserving biodiversity hotspots and protecting endangered species.
- The students learned about the importance of biodiversity conservation in their ecology class.

20. Nanotechnology: Nanoscience, Nanoscale engineering

Definition: The manipulation and control of matter at the nanoscale, typically involving materials or devices with dimensions in the range of 1 to 100 nanometers.

Example:
- Nanotechnology has applications in various fields, including electronics, medicine, and environmental science.
- The study explored the potential of nanotechnology in drug delivery systems for targeted cancer treatment.
- Researchers are investigating the use of nanotechnology to develop more efficient solar cells.
- Nanotechnology offers opportunities for creating lightweight and durable materials with unique properties.
- Ethical considerations surround the potential risks and societal implications of nanotechnology advancements.

5. TECHNOLOGY

1. Innovation: Creativity, Novelty

Definition: The process of introducing new ideas, methods, or technologies to create something original or improve existing products or processes.

Example:

- Technological innovation has revolutionized various industries, including healthcare and communication.
- The company encourages a culture of innovation, allowing employees to propose and implement new ideas.
- The development of electric vehicles is an example of innovation in the automotive industry.
- Innovation plays a vital role in fostering economic growth and competitiveness.
- The start-up's innovative approach to solving a common problem attracted investors.

2. Automation: Mechanization, Robotics

Definition: The use of technology to perform tasks or processes with minimal human intervention.

Example:

- Automation has streamlined manufacturing processes, leading to increased productivity and efficiency.
- The implementation of automated systems reduced human error and improved accuracy in data analysis.
- Many industries are adopting automation to optimize operations and reduce labour costs.
- The rise of artificial intelligence has enabled significant advancements in automation.
- The company invested in automation technology to speed up order processing.

3. Artificial intelligence (AI): Machine intelligence, Cognitive

computing

Definition: The simulation of human intelligence by machines, allowing them to perform tasks that typically require human intelligence, such as problem-solving and decision-making.

Example:

- AI technologies, such as natural language processing and computer vision, are transforming various industries.
- The development of self-driving cars relies on artificial intelligence algorithms for navigation and object recognition.
- AI-powered chatbots provide instant customer support and assistance on websites and mobile applications.
- Ethical considerations arise with the increasing use of AI in decision-making processes.
- The study investigated the ethical implications of AI in healthcare and privacy.

4. Big data: Massive data, Data analytics

Definition: Extremely large and complex data sets that require advanced technologies and analytics for processing and analysis.

Example:

- Big data analytics allows companies to gain insights and make data-driven decisions.
- The study analyzed big data sets to identify patterns and trends in consumer behaviour.
- The collection and analysis of big data can enhance personalized marketing strategies.
- The use of big data in healthcare can lead to improved diagnoses and treatment outcomes.
- Privacy concerns arise with the widespread collection and use of big data by tech companies.

5. Cloud computing: Internet-based computing, Virtualization

Definition: The delivery of computing services, including storage, processing power, and software, over the internet.

Example:

- Cloud computing allows businesses to access and use resources and applications remotely.
- The adoption of cloud computing has reduced infrastructure costs for many organizations.
- Cloud-based storage solutions provide convenient and scalable options for data storage.
- The study explored the security implications of storing sensitive data in the cloud.
- Cloud computing has facilitated remote work and collaboration across geographical locations.

6. Internet of Things (IoT): Connected devices, Smart devices

Definition: The network of physical devices embedded with sensors, software, and connectivity to enable communication and data exchange.
- The IoT allows for seamless connectivity and interaction between devices in various domains, such as smart homes and healthcare.
- IoT devices collect and transmit data for analysis and automation, enhancing efficiency and convenience.
- Security measures must be implemented to protect the privacy of data transmitted through IoT devices.
- The study examined the potential applications of IoT in optimizing energy consumption.
- The growth of IoT technology has spurred the development of smart cities and intelligent infrastructure.

7. Virtual reality (VR): Immersive technology, Simulated reality

Definition: A computer-generated simulation of a three-dimensional environment that can be interacted with and explored by a user.
- Virtual reality technology provides immersive experiences in gaming and entertainment.
- VR training simulations offer a safe and cost-effective method for training professionals in various fields.

- The study investigated the effects of virtual reality therapy in treating phobias and anxiety disorders.
- Virtual reality headsets allow users to explore virtual worlds and interact with virtual objects.
- The potential of virtual reality in enhancing education and remote learning is being explored.

8. Cryptocurrency: Digital currency, Virtual currency

Definition: A digital or virtual form of currency that uses cryptography for secure financial transactions and control of additional unit creation.

Example:
- Cryptocurrencies, such as Bitcoin and Ethereum, have gained popularity as decentralized forms of currency.
- The study explored the potential of blockchain technology in revolutionizing the financial industry through cryptocurrencies.
- Cryptocurrency mining involves solving complex mathematical problems to validate transactions and secure the network.
- The use of cryptocurrencies offers potential benefits, such as faster and more secure cross-border transactions.
- Regulatory frameworks for cryptocurrencies vary across different countries and regions.

10. Cybersecurity: Information security, Data protection

Definition: Measures and practices implemented to protect computer systems, networks, and data from unauthorized access, theft, or damage.

Example:
- Cybersecurity is essential to safeguard sensitive information and prevent cyber-attacks.
- The study investigated the effectiveness of different cybersecurity strategies in preventing data breaches.
- The increasing reliance on digital technologies calls for stronger cybersecurity measures to mitigate risks.

- Individuals and organizations should be vigilant about phishing attempts and employ proper cybersecurity protocols.
- The company invested in cybersecurity training to educate employees on best practices for data protection.

11. Biometrics: Biometric identification, Biometric data
Definition: Measurements or unique physical characteristics used to identify individuals, such as fingerprints, facial features, or iris patterns.
Example:
- Biometric authentication methods, such as fingerprint scanners or facial recognition, enhance security and user convenience.
- The study examined the reliability and accuracy of biometric systems in identity verification.
- Biometric data is increasingly used in border control and airport security to enhance identification processes.
- Privacy concerns arise with the collection and storage of biometric information by government agencies.
- Biometric technology is employed in various sectors, including banking, healthcare, and law enforcement.

12. Internet censorship: Online censorship, Web filtering
Definition: The control or suppression of information and access to certain websites or online content by governments, organizations, or internet service providers.
Example:
- Internet censorship can restrict freedom of expression and limit access to information in certain regions.
- The study analyzed the impact of internet censorship on digital rights and online activism.
- Various countries have implemented internet censorship measures to regulate online content and protect national interests.
- Internet users can employ virtual private networks (VPNs) to bypass internet censorship and access blocked websites.

- The debate surrounding internet censorship involves balancing the need for security with individuals' rights to information access.

13. Nanotechnology: Nanotech, Nanoscience
Definition: The manipulation and control of matter on an atomic, molecular, or supramolecular scale to create functional structures, devices, or materials.
Example:
- Nanotechnology has applications in various fields, including medicine, electronics, and materials science.
- The study investigated the potential of nanotechnology in drug delivery systems for targeted therapies.
- Nanomaterials exhibit unique properties at the nanoscale, leading to advancements in energy storage and sensors.
- Ethical considerations surround the potential environmental and health impacts of nanotechnology.
- Ongoing research focuses on developing scalable and sustainable manufacturing processes for nanomaterials.

14. Biotechnology: Bioengineering, Genetic engineering
Definition: The application of biological systems, organisms, or their components to develop new technologies, products, or processes.
Example:
- Biotechnology plays a vital role in fields such as medicine, agriculture, and environmental science.
- The study explored the potential of biotechnology in developing sustainable biofuels and reducing reliance on fossil fuels.
- Genetic engineering techniques enable the modification of organisms for various purposes, including pharmaceutical production.
- Biotechnology advancements have contributed to the development of vaccines and gene therapies.
- The ethical implications of biotechnology, such as genetically

modified organisms, are subjects of debate and regulation.

15. Optimize: Advance, Develop, Enhance
Definition: To make something as effective, efficient, or functional as possible, often by utilizing technology or analyzing data.
Example:
- Companies employ data analytics to optimize their marketing strategies and target specific customer segments.
- The study focused on optimizing supply chain management through the use of advanced algorithms.
- Website owners optimize their pages to improve search engine rankings and user experience.
- Energy companies use smart grid technologies to optimize electricity distribution and minimize wastage.
- Optimization techniques are employed in logistics to find the most efficient routes for delivery.

16. Streamline: Simplify, Refine
Definition: To make a process or system more efficient and effective by removing unnecessary steps, reducing complexity, or improving workflow.
Example:
- The company implemented new software to streamline its inventory management and reduce costs.
- The study proposed a framework to streamline the recruitment process and improve hiring outcomes.
- Digital transformation initiatives aim to streamline business operations and enhance productivity.
- By adopting agile methodologies, software development teams can streamline the development lifecycle.
- Governments implement regulatory reforms to streamline bureaucratic procedures and facilitate economic growth.

17. Implement: Enforce, Execute, Apply
Definition: To put a plan, idea, or technology into action or practical use.

Example:
- Organizations need to carefully plan and prepare before implementing new software systems.
- The study evaluated the challenges and benefits of implementing artificial intelligence in healthcare.
- Governments implement cybersecurity measures to protect critical infrastructure from cyber threats.
- Companies implement customer relationship management (CRM) systems to improve customer interactions and retention.
- The successful implementation of digital transformation requires strong leadership and change management strategies.

18. Integrate: Incorporate, Combine
Definition: To combine or incorporate different parts, elements, or systems into a unified whole.
Example:
- The company aims to integrate various software applications to improve data sharing and collaboration.
- The study explored the challenges of integrating renewable energy sources into the existing power grid.
- The development team worked to integrate the new module seamlessly with the existing software.
- Businesses strive to integrate customer feedback and preferences into product development processes.
- Integrating artificial intelligence into customer service can enhance response accuracy and efficiency.

19. Develop: Design, Create
Definition: To create, design, or produce something new or improved, often involving research and innovation.
Example:
- Software developers work to develop user-friendly applications with advanced features.
- The study focused on developing sustainable materials for use in electronics manufacturing.
- Companies invest in research and development to develop

cutting-edge technologies and products.
- Developers collaborate to develop open-source software solutions that benefit the community.
- The development of 5G networks promises faster and more reliable communication.

20. Secure: Protect, Fasten

Definition: To protect or make something safe from unauthorized access, damage, or threats.

Example:

- Cybersecurity measures are crucial to secure sensitive data from hackers and cyber attacks.
- The study examined different encryption techniques to secure communication channels.
- Companies implement multi-factor authentication to secure user accounts and prevent unauthorized access.
- Security professionals conduct regular audits to identify and address vulnerabilities in systems.
- The adoption of biometric authentication adds an extra layer of security to access control systems.

6. EDUCATION

1. Pedagogy: Teaching methodology, Instructional techniques
Definition: The theory and practice of teaching, including methods, strategies, and approaches.
Example:
- The school implemented innovative pedagogies to enhance student engagement.
- The study examined the effectiveness of different pedagogical approaches in language learning.
- The teacher employed a student-centred pedagogy, encouraging active participation and critical thinking.
- Online courses often utilize interactive pedagogies to promote learner interaction and collaboration.
- The conference focused on discussing emerging trends and best practices in pedagogy.

2. Curriculum: Syllabus, Course of study
Definition: The subjects, topics, and learning objectives that constitute an educational program.
Example:
- The school revised its curriculum to include more interdisciplinary courses.
- The study analyzed the alignment between the curriculum and the desired learning outcomes.
- The curriculum provides a structured framework for organizing and delivering educational content.
- Teachers collaboratively design the curriculum to ensure coherence and progression.
- The school offers a diverse range of extracurricular activities alongside the formal curriculum.

3. Assessment: Evaluation, Appraisal
Definition: The process of gathering evidence and making

judgments about a student's learning progress or achievement.
Example:
- Teachers use various assessment methods, such as quizzes and projects, to measure student performance.
- The study explored the reliability and validity of different assessment tools for language proficiency.
- Formative assessments provide ongoing feedback to students, helping them identify areas for improvement.
- High-stakes summative assessments determine students' overall achievement and progression.
- The school implemented a comprehensive assessment policy to ensure fairness and consistency.

4. Pedagogical: Educational, Instructional

Definition: Relating to the principles, practices, or methods of teaching and learning.
Example:
- The teacher attended professional development workshops to enhance their pedagogical skills.
- The study investigated the impact of technology on pedagogical practices in mathematics education.
- Pedagogical strategies can be tailored to address the diverse learning needs of students.
- The school adopts a constructivist pedagogical approach, emphasizing hands-on learning experiences.
- Teachers continuously reflect on their pedagogical choices to refine their instructional methods.

5. Literacy: Reading and writing skills, Language proficiency

Definition: The ability to read, write, and comprehend written texts.
Example:
- The literacy rate in the region has improved significantly over the past decade.
- The study examined the relationship between early literacy development and future academic success.

- Digital literacy skills are essential for navigating and critically evaluating online information.
- The school implemented literacy programs to support students with reading difficulties.
- Parents play a crucial role in fostering their children's literacy skills through early exposure to books.

6. Enrolment: Registration, Admission

Definition: The process of officially signing up or registering for a course, program, or educational institution.

Example:
- The enrolment numbers for the university have increased steadily over the years.
- The study analyzed enrolment patterns and demographic trends in higher education.
- Students need to complete the enrolment process before the start of the semester.
- The school offers online enrolment for distance learning programs.
- Late enrolment may incur additional fees or restrictions on course selection.

7. Tutor: Instructor, Mentor

Definition: A person who provides individualized or small-group instruction, guidance, and support to students.
- The tutor helped the student improve their understanding of difficult math concepts.
- The study examined the impact of peer tutoring on student achievement in science subjects.
- The school offers tutoring services to students who need extra academic assistance.
- Online tutoring platforms have become increasingly popular for remote learning.
- The tutor provided valuable feedback and suggestions for improving the student's writing skills.

8. Academic: Educational, Scholarly

Definition: Relating to education, learning, or the pursuit of knowledge, particularly in an institution of higher education.
- The academic year is divided into semesters, each comprising several courses.
- The study investigated the factors that contribute to academic success in university students.
- Academic institutions often have specific criteria for admission into their programs.
- Students are required to meet certain academic standards to maintain their scholarships.
- Academic writing requires a formal tone and adherence to citation and referencing guidelines.

9. Research: Investigation, Study
Definition: The systematic and careful investigation or inquiry into a particular subject or problem to discover new facts or reach new conclusions.
- The researcher conducted extensive research on climate change and its impact on coastal regions.
- The study presented the findings of a research project investigating the effects of sleep deprivation.
- Research skills, such as data analysis and critical thinking, are essential in academic settings.
- The school encourages students to engage in research projects to develop their inquiry skills.
- The research paper highlighted the need for further investigation into the topic.

10. Pedagogue: Teacher, Educator
Definition: A person who specializes in the art or science of teaching; an expert in pedagogy.
- The pedagogue used various teaching techniques to cater to different learning styles.
- The study examined the role of pedagogues in supporting student engagement and learning outcomes.
- Experienced pedagogues are often sought after for their

expertise in instructional strategies.

- The pedagogue employed active learning methods to promote student participation and critical thinking.

- The school invited renowned pedagogues to deliver workshops on effective teaching practices.

11. Knowledgeable: Well-informed, Educated

Definition: Possessing a wide range of knowledge or being well-versed in a particular subject or field.

- The teacher is knowledgeable in various scientific disciplines, which enhances their teaching effectiveness.

- The study relied on the expertise of knowledgeable researchers to analyze the data accurately.

- Students benefit from knowledgeable instructors who can provide in-depth explanations and insights.

- The school offers a comprehensive curriculum taught by knowledgeable faculty members.

- Being knowledgeable in multiple languages opens up opportunities for international communication.

12. Instruction: Teaching, Guidance

Definition: The act of providing knowledge, directions, or information to facilitate learning or accomplish a task.

- The teacher's instructions were clear and easy to follow, enabling students to complete the assignment.

- The study investigated the impact of explicit instruction on vocabulary acquisition.

- Effective instruction incorporates a variety of teaching methods and resources to engage learners.

- The school emphasizes differentiated instruction to cater to the diverse needs of students.

- The instruction manual provides step-by-step guidance on how to assemble the product.

13. Seminar: Workshop, Conference

Definition: A small group or class led by an expert where participants engage in discussions, presentations, or collaborative activities on a specific topic.

- The seminar focused on the latest trends and developments in the field of artificial intelligence.

- The study presented the findings at a national research seminar attended by scholars and experts.

- Students actively participated in the seminar, sharing their ideas and insights with their peers.

- The school organizes regular seminars to foster a

culture of intellectual exchange and growth.

- Attending seminars is a valuable opportunity to expand one's knowledge and network with professionals.

14. Assign: Allocate, Delegate

Definition: To give or designate a task, duty, or responsibility to someone, particularly as part of their educational or professional obligations.

- The teacher assigned a challenging research project to the students to enhance their critical thinking skills.

- The study required participants to complete a questionnaire assigned by the researchers.

- Students should manage their time effectively to meet the deadlines for assigned tasks.

- The school assigns each student a mentor who provides guidance throughout their academic journey.

- The professor assigned readings and reflection papers to stimulate class discussions.

15. Lecture: Presentation, Speech

Definition: An educational talk or speech delivered by an instructor or expert to an audience on a specific subject or topic.

- The lecturer presented a comprehensive overview of the historical events that shaped the modern world.

- The study analyzed the effectiveness of lectures as a teaching method in large classroom settings.

- Students took diligent notes during the lecture to capture important concepts and key points.

- The school invited guest lecturers from industry professionals to share their expertise with students.

- Attending lectures provides an opportunity to gain in-depth knowledge and engage in intellectual discourse.

16. Scholar: Academic, Intellectual

Definition: A person who has gained deep knowledge and expertise in a particular field through study and research.

- The scholar published several influential papers that contributed to the advancement of the field.

- The study acknowledged the contributions of renowned scholars in shaping the theoretical framework.

- The school offers scholarships to attract bright scholars and support their educational pursuits.

- Scholars often collaborate with colleagues from different institutions on research projects.

- The scholar's expertise in the subject matter provided valuable insights during the discussion.

17. Seminar: Workshop, Conference

Definition: A small group or class led by an expert where participants engage in discussions, presentations, or collaborative activities on a specific topic.

- The seminar focused on the latest trends and developments in the field of artificial intelligence.

- The study presented the findings at a national research seminar attended by scholars and experts.

- Students actively participated in the seminar, sharing their ideas and insights with their peers.

- The school organizes regular seminars to foster a culture of intellectual exchange and growth.

- Attending seminars is a valuable opportunity to expand one's knowledge and network with professionals.

18. Lecture: Presentation, Speech

Definition: An educational talk or speech delivered by an instructor or expert to an audience on a specific subject or topic.

- The lecturer presented a comprehensive overview of the historical events that shaped the modern world.
- The study analyzed the effectiveness of lectures as a teaching method in large classroom settings.
- Students took diligent notes during the lecture to capture important concepts and key points.
- The school invited guest lecturers from industry professionals to share their expertise with students.
- Attending lectures provides an opportunity to gain in-depth knowledge and engage in intellectual discourse.

19. Scholar: Academic, Intellectual

Definition: A person who has gained deep knowledge and expertise in a particular field through study and research.
- The scholar published several influential papers that contributed to the advancement of the field.
- The study acknowledged the contributions of renowned scholars in shaping the theoretical framework.
- The school offers scholarships to attract bright scholars and support their educational pursuits.
- Scholars often collaborate with colleagues from different institutions on research projects.
- The scholar's expertise in the subject matter provided valuable insights during the discussion.

20. Dissertation: Thesis, Research paper

Definition: A lengthy and detailed written work that demonstrates a student's research, analysis, and findings in a specific field of study, typically required for the completion of a doctoral degree.
- The student spent years conducting research and writing their dissertation on environmental sustainability.
- The study evaluated the quality of doctoral dissertations across various disciplines.
- Successfully defending the dissertation is a significant milestone in a doctoral candidate's journey.

- The school provides guidance and support to students throughout the dissertation writing process.

- The dissertation committee reviewed and provided feedback on the student's research methodology.

7. SPORTS

1. Competitive: Ambitious, Rivalrous, Fierce
Definition: Showing a strong desire to win or be the best in a competition.
Examples:
- She has a competitive spirit and always gives her best in every game.
- The team's competitive nature drives them to train harder and improve their skills.
- The athletes displayed a fierce determination to win the championship.
- The rivalry between the two teams made for an intense and competitive match.
- He has an ambitious goal of becoming a professional athlete.

2. Score: Tally, Record, Achieve
Definition: To gain points or goals in a game or competition.
Examples:
- The striker scored a brilliant goal from outside the penalty area.
- The team managed to score three goals in the first half of the match.
- He scored high marks in the gymnastics routine, earning him the gold medal.
- The player's excellent performance helped the team score a decisive victory.
- She has scored consistently well in all her tennis matches this season.

3. Athlete: Sportsman/Sportswoman, Competitor, Player
Definition: A person who is skilled in sports and participates in competitive athletic events.
Examples:

- The athletes from various countries gathered to compete in the Olympic Games.
- She has been training rigorously to perform at her best as an athlete.
- The young athlete showed great potential and was scouted by professional scouts.
- The school provides scholarships to exceptional athletes who demonstrate talent and dedication.
- Many athletes rely on a strict diet and fitness regimen to maintain their performance level.

4. Agile: Nimble, Quick, Spry

Definition: Having the ability to move quickly and easily; characterized by quickness and lightness of movement.

Examples:
- The gymnast's agile movements on the balance beam were mesmerizing.
- The soccer player's agility allowed him to navigate through the opposing team's defense.
- The ballet dancer's agile leaps and turns showcased her grace and flexibility.
- The athlete demonstrated his quick reflexes and agile footwork in the boxing ring.
- The team's success can be attributed to their agile defense and swift counterattacks.

5. Compete: Contend, Vie, Battle

Definition: To strive or contend against others in a competition or contest.

Examples:
- The athletes competed fiercely for the gold medal in the 100-meter sprint.
- The two teams will compete against each other in the championship game.
- She decided to compete in the tennis tournament to test her skills against top players.

- The gymnasts have been training hard to compete at the national level.
- The chess players competed in a challenging match that lasted for several hours.

6. Championship: Title, Trophy, Cup
Definition: A prestigious competition or contest to determine the best team or individual in a particular sport.
Examples:
- The team's ultimate goal is to win the championship and bring home the trophy.
- The championship match attracted a large audience and received extensive media coverage.
- The athlete's dedication and hard work paid off when he won the national championship.
- The golf tournament is considered one of the most prestigious championships in the sport.
- The team celebrated their victory in the championship by lifting the trophy high.

7. Fit: Healthy, In shape, Physically active
Definition: In good physical condition, characterized by strength and endurance.
Examples:
- Regular exercise and a balanced diet help to keep the body fit and healthy.
- The coach ensures that the players are fit and ready for the upcoming match.
- She participates in various sports activities to stay fit and maintain her stamina.
- The athlete's rigorous training regime has helped him maintain a fit physique.
- The team's fitness level played a crucial role in their success on the field.

8. Train: Prepare, Coach, Drill
Definition: To engage in systematic practice and exercise to

improve one's skills and physical fitness.

Examples:

- The swimmer trains for several hours every day to improve her technique.

- The coach trains the team rigorously to enhance their tactical understanding of the game.

- He is dedicated to training hard and pushing his limits to achieve his athletic goals.

- The gymnast has been training intensively for months in preparation for the upcoming competition.

- The athlete's commitment to training paid off when he broke the national record.

9. Equipment: Gear, Apparatus, Tools

Definition: The necessary items or gear used in a particular sport or activity.

Examples:

- The soccer player laced up his boots and put on his protective equipment before the match.

- The gym is well-equipped with state-of-the-art fitness equipment.

- The athlete invested in high-quality equipment to enhance his performance.

- The team's equipment manager ensures that all the necessary gear is ready for each game.

- The tennis player carefully selected her racket and other equipment to suit her playing style.

10. Skilled: Talented, Proficient, Competent

Definition: Possessing or demonstrating expertise, proficiency, or ability in a particular sport or activity.

Examples:

- The skilled basketball player effortlessly executed a series of precise dribbling moves.

- The coach recognized the talented and skilled players during the team selection process.

- She has trained for years to become a skilled archer, consistently hitting the bullseye.
- The athlete's years of dedicated practice made her a highly skilled swimmer.
- The team's success can be attributed to their skilled defense and strategic plays.

11. Defend: Protect, Guard, Shield

Definition: To protect one's goal or position from the opposing team or player.

Examples:
- The goalkeeper made an impressive save, defending the team's goal.
- The basketball player used his height and agility to defend against his opponent's shots.
- The team's solid defense prevented the opposing team from scoring any goals.
- The coach emphasized the importance of defending as a team and maintaining a strong defensive line.
- The defender's quick reactions and strong tackles helped neutralize the opponent's attacks.

12. Spectator: Viewer, Observer, Audience

Definition: A person who watches a sports event or performance as a member of the audience.

Examples:
- The stadium was filled with enthusiastic spectators cheering for their favorite team.
- The spectators erupted in applause as the athlete broke the world record.
- She enjoys being a spectator at tennis matches and witnessing the players' incredible skills.
- The event attracted a large number of spectators, creating a lively and vibrant atmosphere.
- The spectators eagerly anticipated the start of the game, eager to see the action unfold.

13. Teamwork: Collaboration, Cooperation, Unity

Definition: The combined effort and cooperation of a group of individuals working together as a team.

Examples:

- The team's success can be attributed to their strong teamwork and effective communication.
- Teamwork is essential in sports like basketball, where players need to coordinate their movements.
- The coach emphasized the importance of teamwork and encouraged players to support one another.
- The team's excellent teamwork was evident in their seamless passing and coordinated plays.
- The project required teamwork, with each member contributing their unique skills and expertise.

14. Challenge: Test, Confront, Push

Definition: To present a difficult or demanding task or situation that requires effort and skill to overcome.

Examples:

- The mountain climber challenged herself to reach the summit of the tallest peak.
- The coach designed a challenging training program to push the athletes to their limits.
- The marathon is a grueling race that challenges runners both physically and mentally.
- The opponent's aggressive playstyle posed a challenge for the tennis player.
- The team embraced the challenge of facing the reigning champions and gave their best effort.

15. Victory: Triumph, Win, Success

Definition: The state of being victorious or winning a competition or game.

Examples:

- The team celebrated their hard-earned victory with cheers and jubilation.

- He experienced a sense of pride and satisfaction after achieving his first victory.
- The athlete's determination and perseverance led her to claim the victory.
- The underdog team staged an incredible comeback and secured a surprising victory.
- The victory in the final match secured their place in the championship.

16. Versatile: Flexible, Adaptable, Multifunctional
Definition: Able to adapt or be used in various sports or activities.
Examples:
- The versatile athlete excels in both swimming and track and field events.
- The tennis player's versatile playing style allows her to perform well on different court surfaces.
- He is a versatile player who can contribute to the team in multiple positions.
- The gymnasium is equipped with versatile exercise machines that target different muscle groups.
- The coach appreciates versatile players who can seamlessly switch between offense and defense.

17. Referee: Officiate, Umpire, Judge
Definition: To act as an official in a sports match, enforcing the rules and making decisions.
Examples:
- The experienced referee carefully monitored the game and made fair calls.
- He was selected to referee the championship match due to his extensive knowledge of the sport.
- The referee's decision to award a penalty kick sparked controversy among the players and spectators.
- The match cannot proceed without a qualified referee to oversee the proceedings.

- The referee intervened to resolve a dispute between two opposing players.

18. Sportsmanship: Fairness, Integrity, Ethical behavior
Definition: Conduct or attitude that embodies fair play, respect, and ethical behavior in sports.
Examples:
- The athlete's sportsmanship was evident when he congratulated his opponent after a tough match.
- The coach emphasized the importance of good sportsmanship and respecting the game's rules.
- She was praised for her display of sportsmanship, even in the face of defeat.
- The team received a sportsmanship award for their exemplary behavior and fair play.
- The spirit of sportsmanship encourages athletes to compete with honor and respect for their opponents.

19. Adjective: Resilient: Tough, Persistent, Tenacious
Definition: Having the ability to recover quickly from setbacks or difficult situations.
Examples:
- The resilient athlete bounced back from a career-threatening injury and returned to competition.
- The team showed resilience by staging a comeback and securing a draw in the final minutes.
- Despite facing numerous challenges, the athlete's resilience allowed him to achieve his goals.
- The coach praised the team's resilience and never-give-up attitude during a challenging season.
- Resilient athletes view setbacks as opportunities for growth and strive to overcome obstacles.

20. Practice: Train, Rehearse, Drill
Definition: To repeatedly perform an activity or exercise in order to improve skills or proficiency.
Examples:

- The gymnast spends hours practicing her routines to perfect her technique.
- The coach encourages the team to practice regularly to enhance their performance.
- He diligently practiced his free-throw shots to improve his accuracy.
- The soccer players gather on the field to practice their passing and coordination.
- The swimmer's consistent practice paid off when she achieved a personal best time.

8. Food and Nutrition

1. Nutrient: Nourishment, Substance, Element
Definition: A substance that provides nourishment, essential for growth and the maintenance of good health.
Examples:
- Fruits and vegetables are rich in essential nutrients like vitamins and minerals.
- The body requires a balance of various nutrients to function properly.
- The nutritionist emphasized the importance of including nutrient-rich foods in the diet.
- The breakfast cereal is fortified with additional nutrients to support overall health.
- The athlete's diet focuses on consuming nutrient-dense foods for optimal performance.

2. Balanced: Healthy, Equitable, Proportionate
Definition: Consisting of a variety of foods that provide a proper combination of nutrients.
Examples:
- A balanced diet includes a mix of carbohydrates, proteins, fats, vitamins, and minerals.
- It's important to maintain a balanced eating pattern to support overall well-being.
- The nutritionist recommended a balanced meal plan that incorporates all food groups.
- The school cafeteria offers balanced meals that meet the nutritional needs of students.
- She strives to maintain a balanced approach to eating, enjoying her favorite foods in moderation.

3. Calorie: Energy unit, Kilojoule, Heat unit
Definition: A unit of measurement used to quantify the amount of energy provided by food and expended through physical activity.

Examples:
- To maintain a healthy weight, it's important to balance calorie intake with calorie expenditure.
- The nutrition label on packaged foods indicates the number of calories per serving.
- The athlete carefully monitors her calorie intake to ensure she meets her energy needs.
- The dietician recommended reducing calorie consumption to promote weight loss.
- A high-calorie diet can contribute to weight gain and other health issues.

4. Organic: Natural, Chemical-free, Pesticide-free
Definition: Produced or grown without the use of synthetic chemicals or pesticides.
Examples:
- Many people prefer organic fruits and vegetables due to their minimal pesticide exposure.
- Organic farming practices prioritize environmental sustainability and natural cultivation methods.
- The grocery store offers a wide selection of organic products, ranging from dairy to grains.
- She shops at a local organic market to support sustainable and eco-friendly food production.
- The organic label ensures that the product meets specific standards for organic certification.

5. Fiber: Roughage, Dietary fiber, Soluble fiber
Definition: A complex carbohydrate found in plant-based foods that aids in digestion and promotes bowel regularity.
Examples:
- Whole grains, fruits, and vegetables are excellent sources of dietary fiber.
- Consuming sufficient fiber can help prevent constipation and promote a healthy digestive system.
- The nutritionist recommended increasing fiber intake to

support heart health.

- The cereal provides a good amount of fiber, keeping you feeling full and satisfied.
- She incorporates fiber-rich foods into her diet, such as beans, lentils, and whole wheat bread.

6. Nutritious: Wholesome, Nourishing, Healthful

Definition: Providing essential nutrients and promoting overall health and well-being.

Examples:

- Leafy greens like spinach and kale are highly nutritious and packed with vitamins.
- The meal replacement shake offers a convenient and nutritious option for busy individuals.
- The dietitian emphasized the importance of consuming a variety of nutritious foods.
- The homemade soup is both delicious and nutritious, containing a mix of vegetables and lean protein.
- The school lunch program aims to provide students with balanced and nutritious meals.

7. Antioxidant: Free-radical scavenger, Radical quencher, Anti-aging agent

Definition: A substance that helps protect the body's cells from damage caused by free radicals.

Examples:

- Berries, dark chocolate, and green tea are rich in antioxidants, which have numerous health benefits.
- The antioxidant properties of certain foods can help reduce the risk of chronic diseases.
- The nutritionist recommended increasing the intake of antioxidant-rich foods for overall health.
- The body produces some antioxidants naturally, but additional sources can be obtained through diet.
- Including a variety of colorful fruits and vegetables ensures a good intake of antioxidants.

8. Consume: Ingest, Eat, Devour

Definition: To take in food, drink, or nutrients into the body by eating or drinking.

Examples:

- It's important to consume a well-balanced diet to meet your nutritional needs.

- The athlete consumes a high-protein meal after intense training to aid in muscle recovery.

- The doctor advised him to consume more fluids to stay hydrated during the hot weather.

- The nutrition label provides information on the number of servings and recommended portion sizes to consume.

- People should be mindful of the amount of added sugar they consume in their diet.

9. Allergen: Irritant, Sensitizing agent, Trigger

Definition: A substance that causes an allergic reaction in individuals with specific sensitivities or allergies.

Examples:

- Peanuts, shellfish, and pollen are common allergens that can elicit allergic responses.

- The school has implemented strict measures to minimize allergen exposure and protect allergic students.

- The doctor conducted allergy tests to identify the specific allergens causing the patient's symptoms.

- It's crucial for individuals with known allergens to read food labels and avoid potential triggers.

- The restaurant provides detailed allergen information to assist customers with dietary restrictions.

10. Wholesome: Nutritious, Healthy, Satisfying

Definition: Conducive to good health and well-being; beneficial for overall nourishment.

Examples:

- The homemade soup is made with wholesome ingredients like fresh vegetables and lean protein.

- The nutritionist recommended incorporating wholesome foods like whole grains and lean meats into the diet.

- The farmer's market offers a variety of wholesome produce grown locally without harmful chemicals.

- She enjoys preparing wholesome meals for her family using organic and natural ingredients.

- The restaurant promotes wholesome eating by using locally sourced, sustainable ingredients.

11. Superfood: Power food, Nutritional powerhouse, Health food

Definition: A nutrient-dense food that is particularly beneficial for health and well-being.

Examples:

- Blueberries, kale, and quinoa are often regarded as superfoods due to their high nutritional content.

- Adding superfoods to your diet can provide a range of vitamins, minerals, and antioxidants.

- The nutritionist recommended incorporating more superfoods into the daily meal plan for added health benefits.

- She starts her day with a smoothie packed with superfoods like spinach, berries, and chia seeds.

- The supermarket offers a dedicated section for superfoods, making it convenient for health-conscious shoppers.

12. Digest: Absorb, Assimilate, Break down

Definition: To break down food in the body and convert it into substances that can be used for energy and growth.

Examples:

- The enzymes in the stomach help digest proteins into smaller molecules for absorption.

- It takes approximately 24 to 72 hours for the body to digest food and eliminate waste.

- Eating slowly and chewing thoroughly aids in the digestion process.

- The doctor suggested incorporating foods rich in dietary

fiber to improve digestion.

- The digestive system plays a crucial role in breaking down food and extracting nutrients.

13. Metabolism: Energy conversion, Biochemical process, Body's engine

Definition: The chemical processes in the body that convert food into energy and enable various bodily functions.

Examples:

- Regular exercise can boost metabolism and help maintain a healthy weight.

- The nutritionist explained the concept of basal metabolic rate, which represents the body's energy expenditure at rest.

- Certain factors, such as age and genetics, can affect an individual's metabolism.

- A balanced diet and sufficient hydration are essential for optimal metabolism.

- The body's metabolism slows down during periods of prolonged fasting or calorie restriction.

14. Organic: Natural, Chemical-free, Pesticide-free

Definition: Grown or produced without the use of synthetic chemicals, pesticides, or genetically modified organisms.

Examples:

- Many health-conscious individuals prefer organic fruits and vegetables to minimize exposure to pesticides.

- The organic farming practices prioritize soil health and sustainability.

- The supermarket offers a wide range of organic products, including dairy, meats, and pantry staples.

- The organic label guarantees that the product meets specific standards for organic certification.

- Choosing organic options supports environmentally friendly and sustainable agricultural practices.

15. Portion: Serving, Helping, Amount

Definition: A specific amount of food intended to be consumed

in one sitting.
Examples:
- The nutritionist advised portion control as part of a healthy eating plan.
- The restaurant offers smaller portion sizes for those who prefer lighter meals.
- It's important to be mindful of portion sizes to prevent overeating.
- The package provides guidelines on recommended portion sizes for optimal nutrition.
- She divided the dish into individual portions to serve to her guests.

16. Wholesome: Nutritious, Healthy, Satisfying
Definition: Conducive to good health and well-being; beneficial for overall nourishment.
Examples:
- The homemade soup is made with wholesome ingredients like fresh vegetables and lean protein.
- The nutritionist recommended incorporating wholesome foods like whole grains and lean meats into the diet.
- The farmer's market offers a variety of wholesome produce grown locally without harmful chemicals.
- She enjoys preparing wholesome meals for her family using organic and natural ingredients.
- The restaurant promotes wholesome eating by using locally sourced, sustainable ingredients.

17. Craving: Longing, Desire, Appetite
Definition: A strong desire or yearning for a specific type of food or drink.
Examples:
- She had a sudden craving for chocolate, so she indulged in a small piece.
- The aroma of freshly baked bread triggered a craving for warm, crusty loaves.

- The pregnant woman experienced intense cravings for pickles and ice cream.
- He couldn't resist the craving for a juicy hamburger, so he treated himself to one.
- After a long day, she satisfied her craving for comfort food by enjoying a bowl of macaroni and cheese.

18. Savor: Enjoy, Relish, Taste
Definition: To fully appreciate and enjoy the flavor or taste of food or drink.
Examples:
- She took her time to savor the rich flavors of the gourmet meal.
- The wine connoisseur savored each sip, noting the subtle nuances of the vintage.
- He savored the aroma of freshly brewed coffee before taking his first sip.
- The chef encouraged the diners to savor the delicate balance of flavors in the dish.
- They gathered around the table to savor the homemade feast prepared with love.

19. Culinary: Cooking, Gastronomic, Epicurean
Definition: Relating to or associated with cooking or the art of preparing food.
Examples:
- The culinary school offers a variety of courses for aspiring chefs and culinary enthusiasts.
- The chef's culinary skills were evident in the beautifully presented and flavorful dishes.
- She enjoys exploring different culinary traditions and experimenting with new recipes.
- The restaurant's menu features a fusion of culinary influences from around the world.
- The culinary competition showcased the talents of aspiring chefs in a high-pressure setting.

20. Nourish: Feed, Sustain, Nurture

Definition: To provide the necessary nutrients and sustenance for growth, health, and well-being.

Examples:

- A well-balanced diet nourishes the body and supports overall health.

- The mother breastfed her baby to nourish and bond with her child.

- The nutritionist recommended incorporating foods that nourish the body with essential vitamins and minerals.

- The soup was made with wholesome ingredients to nourish and comfort the sick patient.

- The community garden project aims to nourish the local population with fresh, locally grown produce.

9. Business

1. Entrepreneur
   Synonyms: Businessperson, Innovator, Founder
   Definition: A person who starts and manages a business, taking on financial risks in the hope of making a profit.
   Examples:
   - Sarah is a successful entrepreneur who founded her own digital marketing agency.
   - Many aspiring entrepreneurs dream of launching a tech startup.
   - The conference featured a panel discussion with renowned entrepreneurs sharing their experiences.
   - The entrepreneur invested her savings into a new business venture.
   - He possesses the entrepreneurial spirit and constantly seeks new business opportunities.

2. Start-up
   Synonyms: New venture, Emerging company, Business launch
   Definition: A newly established business or company, typically with innovative ideas or products.
   Examples:
   - The start-up secured funding from investors to develop its groundbreaking mobile app.
   - Many start-ups face challenges in the early stages of growth but have great potential for success.
   - The start-up scene in the city is vibrant, with numerous innovative ideas being pursued.
   - She joined a start-up as a software engineer and contributed to the development of their flagship product.
   - The government provides support and resources for aspiring entrepreneurs looking to start a new venture.

3. Revenue
   Synonyms: Income, Earnings, Sales

Definition: The total amount of money generated by a business through its activities, such as sales of products or services.

Examples:

- The company's revenue has steadily increased over the past year due to strong product demand.

- The finance department closely monitors the revenue and expenses to ensure financial stability.

- The restaurant experienced a decline in revenue during the off-peak season.

- The company implemented new marketing strategies to boost revenue and attract more customers.

- A comprehensive sales analysis revealed the areas contributing the most to overall revenue.

4. Profit

Synonyms: Earnings, Gain, Net income

Definition: The financial gain realized by a business after deducting expenses from revenue.

Examples:

- The company's cost-cutting measures resulted in higher profits for the fiscal year.

- The CEO announced record-breaking profits, attributing the success to strong market performance.

- The business incurred losses in the initial years but eventually turned a profit.

- The shareholders were pleased with the company's profitability and received attractive dividends.

- The entrepreneur reinvested a portion of the profits into expanding the business.

5. Market

Synonyms: Industry, Marketplace, Sector

Definition: The specific group of consumers or businesses interested in buying a particular product or service.

Examples:

- The company conducted market research to identify the target market for their new smartphone.
- The fashion industry is a highly competitive market with rapidly changing trends.
- The startup identified a gap in the market and developed a unique solution to address the need.
- The marketing team devised a strategy to reach the target market through digital advertising.
- The business expanded its product line to cater to the growing demand in the global market.

6. Investment

Synonyms: Capital, Funding, Stake

Definition: Allocating money or resources into a business, project, or asset with the expectation of achieving a return or benefit.

Examples:
- The venture capitalist made a significant investment in the start-up in exchange for equity.
- The company secured an investment from a prominent angel investor to fuel its expansion plans.
- She diversified her investment portfolio by allocating funds to stocks, bonds, and real estate.
- The business presented its growth projections to attract potential investors.
- The government introduced tax incentives to encourage foreign direct investment in the country.

7. Partnership

Synonyms: Collaboration, Alliance, Joint venture

Definition: A cooperative relationship between two or more individuals or entities working together to achieve mutual goals in business.

Examples:
- The companies formed a strategic partnership to leverage their respective strengths and enter new markets.

- The business owners entered into a partnership agreement outlining the terms and responsibilities.
- The partnership enabled the sharing of resources and expertise, leading to increased productivity.
- The two universities collaborated on a research project through a partnership program.
- The partnership dissolved due to differences in business objectives and management styles.

8. Innovation

Synonyms: Creativity, Novelty, Invention

Definition: The introduction of new ideas, methods, products, or services that result in improved efficiency, competitiveness, or value.

Examples:
- The company encourages a culture of innovation, where employees are encouraged to think outside the box.
- The innovative technology revolutionized the way people communicate and disrupted the market.
- The business invested in research and development to foster innovation and stay ahead of competitors.
- The start-up was recognized for its innovative approach to sustainability, winning several awards.
- The entrepreneur's innovative business model attracted attention from investors and industry experts.

9. Strategy

Synonyms: Plan, Approach, Tactic

Definition: A carefully devised plan of action to achieve long-term goals or objectives in business.

Examples:
- The business implemented a marketing strategy focused on targeting a specific customer segment.
- The CEO outlined the company's growth strategy during the annual shareholders' meeting.
- The business adapted its pricing strategy to gain a

competitive advantage in the market.

- The marketing team developed a social media strategy to enhance brand visibility and engage with customers.
- The business expansion strategy involved opening new stores in key geographic locations.

10. Competition

Synonyms: Rivalry, Contest, Competitiveness

Definition: The act of vying against other businesses or individuals in the market for customers, sales, or market share.

Examples:

- The company faces tough competition from established players in the industry.
- The business conducted a competitive analysis to understand the strengths and weaknesses of competitors.
- The fierce competition in the retail sector prompted the company to innovate and differentiate its offerings.
- The startup entered the market with a unique product, gaining an edge over the competition.
- The business invested in employee training to enhance its competitiveness and customer service.

11. Productivity

Synonyms: Efficiency, Effectiveness, Output

Definition: The measure of how efficiently resources, such as time, labor, or capital, are utilized to produce goods or services.

Examples:

- The business implemented new processes to improve productivity and streamline operations.
- The manager set productivity targets for the team and provided the necessary resources to achieve them.
- The adoption of technology increased productivity and reduced manual errors.
- The company invested in employee well-being programs to enhance motivation and productivity.
- The business analyzed productivity data to identify areas

for improvement and implement corrective measures.

12. Entrepreneurship

Synonyms: Business acumen, Risk-taking, Innovation

Definition: The activity of creating, managing, and taking risks in a business venture with the goal of achieving success.

Examples:

- The entrepreneurship course provided students with practical skills to start their own businesses.
- The entrepreneur's success story inspired others to pursue their entrepreneurial dreams.
- The government launched initiatives to support and encourage entrepreneurship in the region.
- The business incubator offered mentorship and resources to aspiring entrepreneurs.
- She showcased her entrepreneurship skills by launching multiple successful ventures.

13. Corporation

Synonyms: Company, Firm, Organization

Definition: A legal entity formed by individuals or shareholders to conduct business activities, usually with limited liability.

Examples:

- The multinational corporation operates in multiple countries, serving a diverse customer base.
- The corporation's annual report highlighted its financial performance and strategic initiatives.
- The business formed a joint venture with a foreign corporation to expand into new markets.
- The corporation's board of directors oversees major decisions and ensures compliance with regulations.
- She pursued a career in corporate law, working with large corporations on legal matters.

14. Customer

Synonyms: Client, Consumer, Patron

Definition: A person or entity that purchases or uses a product or service offered by a business.

Examples:

- The business focuses on delivering exceptional customer service to build long-term relationships.

- The company conducts customer satisfaction surveys to gather feedback and improve its offerings.

- The business launched a loyalty program to reward its customers for their continued support.

- The customer's feedback prompted the company to make product improvements and address concerns.

- The sales team strives to understand the needs and preferences of each customer to provide personalized solutions.

15. Marketing

Synonyms: Promotion, Advertising, Branding

Definition: The activities and strategies undertaken by a business to promote, sell, and distribute its products or services.

Examples:

- The marketing department developed a comprehensive marketing plan to reach the target audience.

- The business allocated a significant budget for digital marketing campaigns to increase brand awareness.

- The marketing team analyzed market trends and consumer behavior to develop effective marketing strategies.

- The company leveraged social media platforms for targeted marketing and engaging with customers.

- She pursued a career in marketing, specializing in market research and consumer behavior analysis.

16. Collaboration

Synonyms: Cooperation, Partnership, Teamwork

Definition: The act of working together with others to achieve a common goal or complete a task.

Examples:

- The business encouraged collaboration among team

members to foster creativity and innovation.

- The project's success was attributed to the collaboration between different departments.
- The business entered into a collaboration with a renowned designer to create a limited-edition product.
- The team's collaboration and effective communication resulted in the timely completion of the project.
- The company organized workshops and team-building activities to enhance collaboration among employees.

17. Leadership

Synonyms: Management, Guidance, Direction

Definition: The ability to guide and inspire others to achieve a common goal or vision within a business or organization.

Examples:

- The business recognized her leadership skills and promoted her to a managerial position.
- The CEO's strong leadership led the company through a period of rapid growth and expansion.
- The leadership team implemented a new strategic direction to align the business with market trends.
- The business invested in leadership development programs to nurture future leaders within the organization.
- She demonstrated her leadership abilities by successfully leading cross-functional teams on various projects.

18. Ethics

Synonyms: Morality, Integrity, Principles

Definition: The moral principles or values that guide the behavior and actions of individuals or businesses.

Examples:

- The business adheres to a strict code of ethics, ensuring transparency and integrity in its operations.
- The ethics committee reviews and addresses any ethical concerns raised by employees or stakeholders.
- The business practices responsible and ethical sourcing of

materials for its products.

- The CEO emphasized the importance of ethical decision-making and corporate social responsibility.

- She conducted research on business ethics, exploring the impact of ethical behavior on organizational success.

19. Outsourcing

Synonyms: Subcontracting, Externalization, Offshoring

Definition: The practice of contracting a third-party company or individual to perform specific tasks or services

on behalf of a business.

Examples:

- The business outsourced its customer support services to a call center in a different country.

- The company decided to outsource its IT department to reduce costs and improve efficiency.

- The outsourcing of manufacturing operations enabled the business to focus on core competencies.

- The business conducted a cost-benefit analysis before deciding to outsource certain functions.

- She worked as a freelance consultant, offering outsourcing services to small businesses.

20. Risk

Synonyms: Uncertainty, Hazard, Peril

Definition: The potential for loss, harm, or failure associated with a business decision or activity.

Examples:

- The business conducted a risk assessment to identify and mitigate potential risks.

- The entrepreneur took calculated risks to expand the business and enter new markets.

- The business implemented risk management strategies to minimize the impact of potential threats.

- The company faced financial risks due to fluctuations in the market and currency exchange rates.

\- She analyzed the risk-reward ratio before making investment decisions in the stock market.

10. Art and Culture

1. Aesthetic
   Synonyms: Beautiful, Artistic, Pleasing
   Definition: Concerned with or appreciative of beauty, art, or taste.
   Examples:
   - The gallery showcased a variety of aesthetic paintings and sculptures.
   - The artist's work is known for its unique and aesthetic qualities.
   - The interior design of the museum is both functional and aesthetically pleasing.
   - She has a keen eye for aesthetic details in photography.
   - The fashion show displayed a range of aesthetic clothing designs.

2. Masterpiece
   Synonyms: Magnum opus, Chef-d'oeuvre, Gem
   Definition: An outstanding work of art or craft, often regarded as the best of its kind.
   Examples:
   - Leonardo da Vinci's Mona Lisa is considered a masterpiece of Renaissance art.
   - The novel won critical acclaim and is considered the author's masterpiece.
   - The musician's latest album is hailed as a modern masterpiece.
   - The film director's ability to capture emotion on screen is evident in his latest masterpiece.
   - The sculptor's marble statue is regarded as a true masterpiece of sculpting.

3. Sculpture
   Synonyms: Statue, Carving, Figurine
   Definition: Three-dimensional artwork created by shaping or

combining materials such as stone, wood, or metal.

Examples:

- The park is adorned with various sculptures created by renowned artists.

- The museum houses an extensive collection of ancient and contemporary sculptures.

- The sculptor used clay to create a small-scale model of the sculpture before carving it in marble.

- The public square features a large bronze sculpture as a focal point.

- She enrolled in a sculpting class to learn the techniques of creating sculptures.

4. Exhibit

Synonyms: Display, Show, Presentation

Definition: A public display of artwork or objects of interest for viewing and appreciation.

Examples:

- The art gallery is hosting an exhibit showcasing local artists' works.

- The museum's new exhibit explores the history of ancient civilizations.

- The artist was invited to exhibit his paintings at a prestigious art fair.

- Visitors were captivated by the photography exhibit's thought-provoking images.

- She submitted her sculpture to be considered for the upcoming art exhibit.

5. Performance

Synonyms: Show, Presentation, Act

Definition: An act or display of artistic or creative skill in front of an audience.

Examples:

- The theater company put on a captivating performance of Shakespeare's Hamlet.

- The ballet performance received a standing ovation from the audience.
- The musician's live performance was energetic and engaging.
- The circus troupe delivered an impressive performance of acrobatics and stunts.
- She rehearsed diligently to deliver a flawless dance performance.

6. Expression
   Synonyms: Articulation, Manifestation, Communication
   Definition: The act of conveying thoughts, emotions, or ideas through various forms of art or communication.
   Examples:
   - The painting is a powerful expression of the artist's inner emotions.
   - The poet's words were a beautiful expression of love and longing.
   - The dancer's movements were a graceful expression of joy and freedom.
   - The actor's performance was a compelling expression of grief and despair.
   - She used photography as a means of self-expression and storytelling.

7. Heritage
   Synonyms: Legacy, Tradition, Inheritance
   Definition: Cultural or historical traditions, beliefs, customs, or artifacts that are passed down through generations.
   Examples:
   - The country's rich heritage is reflected in its architecture and traditions.
   - The museum preserves and showcases the cultural heritage of the indigenous people.
   - The festival celebrates the community's cultural heritage through music and dance.

- The artist drew inspiration from her cultural heritage to create unique artworks.
- She embarked on a journey to discover her family's heritage and roots.

8. Renaissance

Synonyms: Rebirth, Revival, Renewal

Definition: A period of renewed interest, growth, or activity in the arts, literature, and sciences.

Examples:

- The Renaissance era in Europe witnessed significant advancements in art, science, and philosophy.
- The museum houses a collection of Renaissance paintings by renowned artists.
- The play reflects the spirit of the Renaissance through its exploration of humanism and intellectual curiosity.
- The Renaissance architecture of the cathedral is characterized by its ornate details and grandeur.
- She studied the works of Renaissance masters to understand their techniques and style.

9. Cultural

Synonyms: Ethnic, Traditional, Social

Definition: Relating to the customs, beliefs, practices, and traditions of a particular group or society.

Examples:

- The city is known for its diverse cultural heritage and vibrant arts scene.
- The museum offers workshops that provide visitors with a deeper understanding of cultural traditions.
- The dance performance showcased a fusion of different cultural influences.
- She is deeply interested in learning about various cultural practices from around the world.
- The novel explores the complexities of cultural identity and belonging.

10. Abstract

Synonyms: Nonrepresentational, Conceptual, Symbolic

Definition: Artistic or creative work that does not attempt to represent an accurate depiction of reality but instead focuses on concepts, emotions, or ideas.

Examples:

- The abstract painting evoked a sense of mystery and intrigue.
- The artist used bold colors and geometric shapes to create abstract compositions.
- The writer's poetry often explores abstract themes such as love and existentialism.
- The dancer's movements were fluid and abstract, conveying a range of emotions.
- She appreciated the abstract nature of modern art and its ability to evoke thought and emotion.

11. Genre

Synonyms: Category, Style, Type

Definition: A specific category or classification of artistic or literary works that share similar characteristics, themes, or styles.

Examples:

- The library has a wide selection of books spanning different genres, from romance to science fiction.
- The film festival features films of various genres, including comedy, drama, and documentary.
- The musician's latest album blends elements from multiple genres, creating a unique sound.
- The artist experiments with different genres, from realistic portraits to abstract landscapes.
- She enjoys reading books from the fantasy genre, immersing herself in imaginary worlds.

12. Impression

Synonyms: Impact, Influence, Effect

Definition: A strong and lasting effect or feeling produced by an artistic or sensory experience.

Examples:

- The artist's brushstrokes created a vivid impression of movement and energy.

- The performance left a lasting impression on the audience with its powerful storytelling.

- The musician's soulful singing made a profound impression on listeners.

- The play's thought-provoking dialogue sparked a deep impression of introspection.

- She visited an art exhibition and was left with a lasting impression of the artist's talent.

13. Symbolism

Synonyms: Representation, Significance, Meaning

Definition: The use of symbols to represent ideas, qualities, or concepts in art, literature, or communication.

Examples:

- The butterfly in the painting is often interpreted as a symbol of transformation and rebirth.

- The novel's use of recurring motifs and symbols adds depth and layers of meaning to the story.

- The artist incorporated religious symbolism in the mural, conveying spiritual themes.

- The filmmaker used color symbolism to evoke specific emotions and moods in the movie.

- She analyzed the poem's symbolism to uncover hidden messages and themes.

14. Critique

Synonyms: Analysis, Evaluation, Review

Definition: A detailed assessment or examination of a work of art or literature, highlighting its strengths, weaknesses, and artistic merits.

Examples:

- The art professor provided constructive critiques to help students improve their artwork.
- The film received mixed critiques from movie critics, with some praising its storytelling and others criticizing its pacing.
- The writer submitted her manuscript to a literary magazine for critique and feedback.
- The theater group held a panel discussion to engage in a critical critique of the play.
- She appreciated receiving honest critiques from fellow artists to grow and refine her skills.

15. Interpretation

Synonyms: Understanding, Explanation, Analysis

Definition: The act of comprehending or explaining the meaning, significance, or intention behind a work of art or cultural expression.

Examples:
- The art exhibition encouraged visitors to form their own interpretations of the artwork.
- The book's ambiguous ending allows for different interpretations among readers.
- The dancer's performance was open to interpretation, leaving room for individual experiences.
- The museum guide provided insightful interpretations of the historical artifacts on display.
- She shared her interpretation of the poem, exploring its themes and underlying messages.

16. Patron

Synonyms: Sponsor, Supporter, Benefactor

Definition: An individual or organization that provides financial or other support to artists, performers, or cultural institutions.

Examples:
- The wealthy philanthropist became a patron of the arts, funding various cultural initiatives.

- The company acted as a patron for emerging musicians, offering recording contracts and promotional support.
- The local government allocated funds to support local artists and become patrons of the community.
- The museum relies on patrons' donations to acquire new artworks and maintain its collections.
- She thanked her patrons for their ongoing support and belief in her artistic vision.

17. Folklore
Synonyms: Traditional stories, Myths, Legends
Definition: Traditional customs, beliefs, stories, and practices passed down through generations within a particular culture or community.
Examples:
- The country's folklore is rich with tales of mythical creatures and heroic adventures.
- The storyteller captivated the audience with ancient folklore about the origins of their village.
- The festival celebrates the region's folklore through traditional dances, music, and storytelling.
- The writer drew inspiration from local folklore to create a fictional world for her novel.
- She enjoys reading folklore from different cultures to learn about their traditional beliefs and values.

18. Curator
Synonyms: Keeper, Manager, Organizer
Definition: A person responsible for managing and overseeing collections of artworks, artifacts, or exhibitions in a museum or gallery.
Examples:
- The museum curator carefully selects and curates exhibits to provide a meaningful experience for visitors.
- The art gallery appointed a new curator to bring fresh perspectives to its collection.

- The curator organized a retrospective exhibition showcasing the works of a renowned painter.
- The archaeology museum's curator conducted extensive research on ancient civilizations.
- She aspires to become a museum curator to curate and showcase artworks from diverse cultures.

19. Exhibition
Synonyms: Display, Show, Presentation
Definition: A public display of artworks, artifacts, or objects of interest for viewing and appreciation.
Examples:
- The art museum hosted a special exhibition featuring the works of contemporary artists.
- The photography exhibition highlighted the beauty of nature through stunning images.
- The science museum's interactive exhibition engaged visitors in hands-on learning experiences.
- The artist was invited to participate in a group exhibition showcasing emerging talents.
- She visited an exhibition of historical artifacts, gaining insight into the region's past.

20. Heritage
Synonyms: Legacy, Tradition, Inheritance
Definition: Cultural or historical traditions, beliefs, customs, or artifacts that are passed down through generations.
Examples:
- The city's architectural heritage is preserved in its historic buildings and landmarks.
- The festival celebrates the community's rich heritage through music, dance, and cuisine.
- The museum's collection represents the cultural heritage of diverse communities.
- The artist draws inspiration from her cultural heritage, incorporating traditional motifs into her artwork.

- She takes pride in her heritage and actively promotes cultural awareness and understanding.

11. History

1. Ancient
   Synonyms: Old, Antique, Prehistoric
   Definition: Belonging to a period of history that is far in the past, typically before the Middle Ages.
   Examples:
   - The archaeologists discovered ancient artifacts buried deep in the ruins.
   - The ancient civilization left behind impressive architectural structures.
   - She studied ancient history to understand the origins of human civilization.
   - The ancient Egyptians built magnificent pyramids as tombs for their pharaohs.
   - The museum houses a collection of ancient Greek pottery.

2. Civilization
   Synonyms: Society, Culture, Civilization
   Definition: A complex and organized society marked by advancements in art, science, technology, and social structure.
   Examples:
   - The Indus Valley civilization flourished thousands of years ago.
   - The Mayan civilization had a sophisticated system of writing and mathematics.
   - She researched the ancient civilizations of Mesopotamia and their contributions.
   - The museum exhibits artifacts from various ancient civilizations.
   - The professor gave a lecture on the rise and fall of ancient civilizations.

3. Empire
   Synonyms: Kingdom, Realm, Dominion
   Definition: A group of territories or nations ruled by a single

supreme authority, typically an emperor or empress.
Examples:
- The Roman Empire spanned across Europe, Asia, and Africa.
- The Ottoman Empire was a powerful force in the Middle East for centuries.
- She studied the military strategies employed by ancient empires.
- The history textbook explores the rise and decline of different empires.
- The emperor's palace was a symbol of the empire's grandeur and power.

4. Revolution
Synonyms: Uprising, Rebellion, Insurrection
Definition: A sudden and significant change or transformation, often involving political, social, or economic aspects.
Examples:
- The French Revolution marked a turning point in European history.
- The Industrial Revolution brought about profound changes in manufacturing and transportation.
- She wrote an essay on the impact of the digital revolution on modern society.
- The revolution resulted in the overthrow of the oppressive regime.
- The revolutionaries fought for equality and justice for all.

5. Dynasty
Synonyms: Monarchy, Regime, Ruling family
Definition: A succession of rulers from the same family, often with power being passed down through generations.
Examples:
- The Ming Dynasty ruled China for nearly three centuries.
- The Romanov Dynasty governed Russia for over 300 years.
- She studied the achievements and cultural contributions of

the Tang Dynasty.
- The dynasty's decline was marked by political instability and economic challenges.
- The royal palace was the center of power during the reign of the dynasty.

6. Archaeology
Synonyms: Excavation, Antiquities, Study of the past
Definition: The scientific study of past human societies and cultures through the analysis of artifacts, structures, and remains.
Examples:
- The archaeologists carefully excavated the ancient burial site.
- She pursued a career in archaeology to uncover mysteries of the past.
- The museum curator specializes in ancient artifacts and archaeological finds.
- The archaeology team discovered a lost city buried beneath the desert sands.
- The excavation revealed valuable insights into the daily lives of ancient civilizations.

7. Renaissance
Synonyms: Rebirth, Revival, Renewal
Definition: A period of renewed interest, growth, or activity in the arts, literature, and sciences.
Examples:
- The Renaissance era in Europe witnessed significant advancements in art, science, and philosophy.
- The museum houses a collection of Renaissance paintings by renowned artists.
- She wrote a research paper on the cultural impact of the Renaissance.
- The Renaissance period marked a shift towards humanism and individualism.

- The architecture of the time reflected the ideals of the Renaissance.

8. Monarchy
   Synonyms: Kingdom, Sovereignty, Royalty
   Definition: A form of government in which a single ruler, such as a king or queen, holds supreme authority.
   Examples:
   - The British monarchy has a long history dating back centuries.
   - The monarchy's power was gradually diminished with the rise of democracy.
   - She studied the different monarchies in Europe and their roles in shaping history.
   - The palace served as the official residence of the monarchy.
   - The coronation ceremony symbolizes the ascension of a monarch to the throne.

9. Revolution
   Synonyms: Uprising, Rebellion, Insurrection
   Definition: A sudden and significant change or transformation, often involving political, social, or economic aspects.
   Examples:
   - The French Revolution marked a turning point in European history.
   - The Industrial Revolution brought about profound changes in manufacturing and transportation.
   - She wrote an essay on the impact of the digital revolution on modern society.
   - The revolution resulted in the overthrow of the oppressive regime.
   - The revolutionaries fought for equality and justice for all.

10. Dynasty
   Synonyms: Monarchy, Regime, Ruling family
   Definition: A succession of rulers from the same family, often

with power being passed down through generations.
Examples:
- The Ming Dynasty ruled China for nearly three centuries.
- The Romanov Dynasty governed Russia for over 300 years.
- She studied the achievements and cultural contributions of the Tang Dynasty.
- The dynasty's decline was marked by political instability and economic challenges.
- The royal palace was the center of power during the reign of the dynasty.

11. Archaeology
Synonyms: Excavation, Antiquities, Study of the past
Definition: The scientific study of past human societies and cultures through the analysis of artifacts, structures, and remains.
Examples:
- The archaeologists carefully excavated the ancient burial site.
- She pursued a career in archaeology to uncover mysteries of the past.
- The museum curator specializes in ancient artifacts and archaeological finds.
- The archaeology team discovered a lost city buried beneath the desert sands.
- The excavation revealed valuable insights into the daily lives of ancient civilizations.

12. Renaissance
Synonyms: Rebirth, Revival, Renewal
Definition: A period of renewed interest, growth, or activity in the arts, literature, and sciences.
Examples:
- The Renaissance era in Europe witnessed significant advancements in art, science, and philosophy.
- The museum houses a collection of Renaissance paintings

by renowned artists.

- She wrote a research paper on the cultural impact of the Renaissance.

- The Renaissance period marked a shift towards humanism and individualism.

- The architecture of the time reflected the ideals of the Renaissance.

13. Monarchy

Synonyms: Kingdom, Sovereignty, Royalty

Definition: A form of government in which a single ruler, such as a king or queen, holds supreme authority.

Examples:

- The British monarchy has a long history dating back centuries.

- The monarchy's power was gradually diminished with the rise of democracy.

- She studied the different monarchies in Europe and their roles in shaping history.

- The palace served as the official residence of the monarchy.

- The coronation ceremony symbolizes the ascension of a monarch to the throne.

14. Renaissance

Synonyms: Rebirth, Revival, Renewal

Definition: A period of renewed interest, growth, or activity in the arts, literature, and sciences.

Examples:

- The Renaissance era in Europe witnessed significant advancements in art, science, and philosophy.

- The museum houses a collection of Renaissance paintings by renowned artists.

- She wrote a research paper on the cultural impact of the Renaissance.

- The Renaissance period marked a shift towards humanism and individualism.

- The architecture of the time reflected the ideals of the Renaissance.

15. Monarchy
Synonyms: Kingdom, Sovereignty, Royalty
Definition: A form of government in which a single ruler, such as a king or queen, holds supreme authority.
Examples:
- The British monarchy has a long history dating back centuries.
- The monarchy's power was gradually diminished with the rise of democracy.
- She studied the different monarchies in Europe and their roles in shaping history.
- The palace served as the official residence of the monarchy.
- The coronation ceremony symbolizes the ascension of a monarch to the throne.

16. Renaissance
Synonyms: Rebirth, Revival, Renewal
Definition: A period of renewed interest, growth, or activity in the arts, literature, and sciences.
Examples:
- The Renaissance era in Europe witnessed significant advancements in art, science, and philosophy.
- The museum houses a collection of Renaissance paintings by renowned artists.
- She wrote a research paper on the cultural impact of the Renaissance.
- The Renaissance period marked a shift towards humanism and individualism.
- The architecture of the time reflected the ideals of the Renaissance.

17. Monarchy
Synonyms: Kingdom, Sovereignty, Royalty
Definition: A form of government in which a single ruler,

such as a king or queen, holds supreme authority.

Examples:

- The British monarchy has a long history dating back centuries.

- The monarchy's power was gradually diminished with the rise of democracy.

- She studied the different monarchies in Europe and their roles in shaping history.

- The palace served as the official residence of the monarchy.

- The coronation ceremony symbolizes the ascension of a monarch to the throne.

18. Archaeology

Synonyms: Excavation, Antiquities, Study of the past

Definition: The scientific study of past human societies and cultures through the analysis of artifacts, structures, and remains.

Examples:

- The archaeologists carefully excavated the ancient burial site.

- She pursued a career in archaeology to uncover mysteries of the past.

- The museum curator specializes in ancient artifacts and archaeological finds.

- The archaeology team discovered a lost city buried beneath the desert sands.

- The excavation revealed valuable insights into the daily lives of ancient civilizations.

19. Renaissance

Synonyms: Rebirth, Revival, Renewal

Definition: A period of renewed interest, growth, or activity in the arts, literature, and sciences.

Examples:

- The Renaissance era in Europe witnessed significant advancements in art, science, and philosophy.

- The museum houses a collection of Renaissance paintings by renowned artists.

- She wrote a research paper on the cultural impact of the Renaissance.

- The Renaissance period marked a shift towards humanism and individualism.

- The architecture of the time reflected the ideals of the Renaissance.

20. Monarchy

Synonyms: Kingdom, Sovereignty, Royalty

Definition: A form of government in which a single ruler, such as a king or queen, holds supreme authority.

Examples:

- The British monarchy has a long history dating back centuries.

- The monarchy's power was gradually diminished with the rise of democracy.

- She studied the different monarchies in Europe and their roles in shaping history.

- The palace served as the official residence of the monarchy.

- The coronation ceremony symbolizes the ascension of a monarch to the throne.

12. Politics and Government

1. Democracy
   Synonyms: Republic, Self-government, Rule by the people
   Definition: A system of government in which power is vested in the people, who exercise it through elected representatives.
   Examples:
   - The country transitioned from a dictatorship to a democracy after a long struggle.
   - Citizens have the right to vote and participate in the democratic process.
   - Democracy promotes equality and protects individual rights.
   - The election was held to determine the new democratic leader.
   - The principles of democracy include transparency and accountability.

2. Legislation
   Synonyms: Lawmaking, Statute, Act
   Definition: The process of making or enacting laws by a legislative body.
   Examples:
   - The parliament passed new legislation to address the issue of climate change.
   - The legislation aims to protect consumers from fraudulent practices.
   - Lawmakers proposed a bill for stricter gun control legislation.
   - The government introduced legislation to promote economic growth.
   - The president signed the legislation into law.

3. Governance
   Synonyms: Administration, Rule, Management
   Definition: The act or manner of governing or exercising authority.

Examples:
- Good governance requires transparency and accountability.
- The governance of the organization is overseen by a board of directors.
- The political party promised to improve governance and reduce corruption.
- The governance structure ensures checks and balances on power.
- Effective governance is essential for a stable society.

4. Constitution

Synonyms: Charter, Framework, Fundamental law

Definition: A set of fundamental principles or established precedents that guide the governance of a nation or organization.

Examples:
- The constitution guarantees the rights and freedoms of citizens.
- The court interpreted the constitution to protect individual liberties.
- Amendments to the constitution require a rigorous process.
- The constitution outlines the powers and limitations of the government.
- The constitutional rights of the accused must be upheld.

5. Bureaucracy

Synonyms: Administration, Red tape, Officialdom

Definition: A system of government or organization characterized by complex hierarchical structures, excessive rules, and slow decision-making processes.

Examples:
- The bureaucracy is often criticized for its inefficiency and lack of responsiveness.
- Navigating the bureaucratic procedures can be time-consuming.
- The government aims to streamline the bureaucracy to

improve efficiency.

- Bureaucratic red tape hinders the progress of important projects.

- The organization is burdened by a bloated bureaucracy.

6. Diplomacy

Synonyms: Negotiation, Tact, Foreign relations

Definition: The art and practice of conducting negotiations and maintaining relations between nations or groups.

Examples:

- Diplomacy plays a crucial role in resolving international conflicts.

- Skilled diplomats engage in diplomatic negotiations to foster peace.

- The ambassador's diplomatic skills helped strengthen bilateral ties.

- Diplomatic efforts were made to secure a trade agreement.

- The country employs a team of diplomats to represent its interests abroad.

7. Policy

Synonyms: Strategy, Plan, Course of action

Definition: A principle, course of action, or set of guidelines adopted or pursued by a government, organization, or individual.

Examples:

- The government implemented a new policy to stimulate economic growth.

- The policy aims to promote renewable energy sources and reduce carbon emissions.

- The school has a policy of zero tolerance for bullying.

- The organization's policy on diversity and inclusion is widely praised.

- The policy had a significant impact on public health outcomes.

8. Opposition

Synonyms: Resistance, Dissent, Rivalry

Definition: The political party or group that opposes the ruling party or government.

Examples:

- The opposition criticized the government's handling of the economy.
- The opposition leader voiced concerns over human rights violations.
- The opposition party called for a vote of no confidence against the prime minister.
- The opposition staged protests to demand political reforms.
- The opposition gained support ahead of the upcoming elections.

9. Corruption

Synonyms: Bribery, Fraud, Nepotism

Definition: Dishonest or unethical behavior by individuals in positions of power, typically involving the abuse of public resources or authority for personal gain.

Examples:

- The government launched an anti-corruption campaign to root out systemic bribery.
- The investigation uncovered widespread corruption within the police department.
- Corruption erodes public trust and undermines democracy.
- The corrupt official was arrested for embezzling public funds.
- Transparency and accountability measures are crucial in combating corruption.

10. Autonomy

Synonyms: Independence, Self-governance, Sovereignty

Definition: The right or condition of self-government or independence.

Examples:

- The region fought for autonomy from the central

government.

- Indigenous communities strive to preserve their cultural autonomy.

- The decision grants more autonomy to local authorities.

- The country gained autonomy after years of colonization.

- Autonomy allows individuals or groups to make decisions based on their own principles.

11. Legislature

Synonyms: Congress, Parliament, Lawmaking body

Definition: A deliberative body with the power to make laws, usually consisting of elected representatives.

Examples:

- The legislature passed a bill to reform the education system.

- The members of the legislature debated the proposed tax legislation.

- The opposition party introduced a motion in the legislature to address social inequality.

- The legislature plays a vital role in shaping public policy.

- The governor signed the legislation into law after it was approved by the legislature.

12. Federalism

Synonyms: Devolution, Decentralization, Distribution of power

Definition: A system of government in which power is divided between a central authority and regional or state governments.

Examples:

- Federalism allows for a balance of power between the national and state governments.

- The country adopted a federalism model to accommodate regional differences.

- The federalist system ensures that certain powers are reserved for the central government.

- Federalism allows for greater local autonomy and decision-making.

- The debate over federalism versus centralism is ongoing.

13. Electorate

Synonyms: Voters, Constituents, Citizens

Definition: The body of people who are entitled to vote in an election.

Examples:

- The candidates campaigned vigorously to win the support of the electorate.

- Voter turnout among the electorate was high in the last election.

- The government promised to address the concerns of the electorate.

- The electorate expressed their dissatisfaction with the current administration through their votes.

- The candidate's policies resonated with a large segment of the electorate.

14. Ideology

Synonyms: Belief system, Philosophy, Weltanschauung

Definition: A set of ideas, beliefs, or principles that form the basis of a political or economic theory or system.

Examples:

- Different political parties often have distinct ideologies.

- The politician's ideology aligns with conservative values.

- The ideology of socialism advocates for a more equitable distribution of wealth.

- The candidate presented a comprehensive ideology for economic development.

- Ideology shapes the policies and actions of political leaders.

15. Civil liberties

Synonyms: Freedoms, Rights, Constitutional rights

Definition: Basic rights and freedoms that are guaranteed to individuals by law, typically in the context of a democratic society.

Examples:
- The constitution protects civil liberties such as freedom of speech and religion.
- The government must respect and uphold the civil liberties of its citizens.
- The organization advocates for the preservation of civil liberties for all individuals.
- The court ruled that the legislation violated the defendant's civil liberties.
- Civil liberties are essential for the functioning of a democratic society.

16. Diplomat
Synonyms: Ambassador, Envoy, Representative
Definition: A person who is appointed by a government to conduct official negotiations and maintain relations with other countries or international organizations.
Examples:
- The diplomat negotiated a trade agreement between the two nations.
- The diplomat's role is to represent the interests of their home country abroad.
- The ambassador is a high-ranking diplomat responsible for diplomatic relations.
- The diplomat participated in peace talks to resolve the conflict.
- Diplomats engage in diplomatic discussions to address global issues.

17. Coalition
Synonyms: Alliance, Union, Partnership
Definition: An alliance or partnership formed by different political parties or groups with a common goal or objective.
Examples:
- The coalition government was formed after the election to ensure stability.

- Political parties joined forces to form a coalition against the ruling party.
- The coalition advocates for environmental policies and sustainability.
- The coalition of organizations worked together to address social inequality.
- The coalition's policies attracted a diverse range of supporters.

18. Referendum

Synonyms: Plebiscite, Popular vote, Ballot

Definition: A direct vote in which the entire electorate is invited to vote on a particular issue or proposal.

Examples:

- The government held a referendum on whether to legalize same-sex marriage.
- The referendum resulted in a majority in favor of leaving the European Union.
- The decision to increase taxes was subject to a referendum.
- The referendum allowed citizens to have a say in important policy matters.
- The outcome of the referendum will shape the future of the country.

19. Ombudsman

Synonyms: Mediator, Arbitrator, Advocate

Definition: An official appointed to investigate and resolve complaints or disputes between individuals and the government or public institutions.

Examples:

- The ombudsman investigates complaints of maladministration by government officials.
- The ombudsman acts as a neutral mediator in resolving disputes between citizens and public institutions.
- The ombudsman provides an avenue for individuals to voice their concerns and seek redress.

- The role of the ombudsman is to ensure transparency and fairness in the government's actions.
- The ombudsman's report highlighted instances of corruption within the police force.

20. Secularism

Synonyms: Non-religious, Laicism, Irreligion

Definition: The principle or belief that government and societal institutions should be separate from religious institutions, and that public affairs should be conducted without influence from religious beliefs.

Examples:

- The country upholds secularism as a fundamental principle of governance.
- Secularism ensures religious freedom and prevents discrimination based on faith.
- The debate over the role of religion in public schools centers around the principle of secularism.
- Secularism promotes equality and protects the rights of individuals with different beliefs.
- The constitution guarantees the practice of secularism in state affairs.

13. Literature

1. Protagonist
   Synonyms: Main character, Hero, Lead
   Definition: The central character in a literary work, often portrayed as the hero or main focus of the story.
   Examples:
   - The protagonist overcame numerous obstacles to achieve their goals.
   - In the novel, the protagonist embarks on a journey of self-discovery.
   - The audience sympathized with the struggles faced by the protagonist.
   - The author developed the protagonist's character arc throughout the story.
   - The protagonist's actions drove the plot forward.

2. Antagonist
   Synonyms: Villain, Adversary, Foe
   Definition: The character or force that opposes the protagonist in a literary work.
   Examples:
   - The antagonist's sinister intentions created tension in the story.
   - The protagonist and antagonist engaged in a fierce battle of wits.
   - The antagonist's actions served as obstacles for the main character.
   - The author depicted the antagonist as a complex and multifaceted character.
   - The resolution of the conflict depended on the protagonist overcoming the antagonist.

3. Symbolism
   Synonyms: Allegory, Metaphor, Representation
   Definition: The use of symbols to represent ideas or qualities,

often giving deeper meaning to a literary work.

Examples:

- The author used the color red as a symbol of passion and love.

- The recurring motif of the bird symbolized freedom and hope.

- The crumbling mansion symbolized the decay of the aristocracy.

- The use of light and darkness symbolized the contrast between good and evil.

- The symbol of the rose represented beauty and fragility.

4. Foreshadowing

Synonyms: Prefiguring, Anticipation, Prolepsis

Definition: The literary technique of hinting or suggesting future events or outcomes in a story.

Examples:

- The ominous music foreshadowed the impending danger.

- The author strategically inserted subtle clues to foreshadow the plot twist.

- The dream sequence served as a foreshadowing of the character's destiny.

- The weather conditions foreshadowed an approaching storm.

- The early mention of a mysterious character foreshadowed their later significance.

5. Metaphor

Synonyms: Analogy, Comparison, Figure of speech

Definition: A figure of speech that describes one thing in terms of another, highlighting a similarity between the two.

Examples:

- Her laughter was music to my ears, a melody that brought joy to my heart.

- Time is a thief, stealing away the moments we hold dear.

- His words were a soothing balm, healing the wounds of the

past.
- The classroom was a zoo, chaotic and filled with noise.
- Love is a battlefield, where hearts are won and lost.

6. Irony
Synonyms: Satire, Paradox, Contradiction
Definition: A literary technique that involves a contrast between what is expected or intended and what actually happens or is said.
Examples:
- The millionaire who lived in a small, rundown house was a prime example of irony.
- The weather forecast predicted sunshine, but it rained all day —how ironic.
- His words of wisdom were met with laughter, a cruel twist of irony.
- The thief was caught stealing from the police station, a truly ironic situation.
- The failed comedian who made everyone else laugh but never found joy himself—such irony.

7. Imagery
Synonyms: Descriptive language, Figurative language, Visual representation
Definition: The use of vivid and descriptive language to create mental images and evoke sensory experiences in the reader's mind.
Examples:
- The writer's rich imagery painted a vibrant picture of the sunset over the horizon.
- The scent of freshly baked bread filled the air, invoking memories of warmth and comfort.
- The author's detailed imagery brought the bustling city to life on the page.
- The dew-covered grass sparkled like diamonds in the morning light.

- The roaring waves crashed against the rugged cliffs, their power and force palpable.

8. Alliteration

Synonyms: Repetition of sound, Tongue twister, Consonance

Definition: The repetition of the same consonant sounds, usually at the beginning of closely connected words.

Examples:
- Peter Piper picked a peck of pickled peppers.
- She sells seashells by the seashore.
- The big, brown bear bounded through the bushes.
- The slippery snake silently slithered across the sand.
- The twinkling stars twinkled in the midnight sky.

9. Theme

Synonyms: Central idea, Motif, Subject

Definition: The main underlying message or central topic explored in a literary work.

Examples:
- The theme of love and sacrifice permeated throughout the novel.
- The author explored the theme of power and corruption in society.
- The story's theme of redemption resonated with readers.
- The theme of identity and self-discovery was a prominent element in the play.
- The film delved into the theme of human resilience in the face of adversity.

10. Prose

Synonyms: Writing, Text, Composition

Definition: Written or spoken language in its ordinary form, without metrical structure, as distinguished from poetry.

Examples:
- The author's beautiful prose captivated the readers.
- She excelled in writing both poetry and prose.
- The essay was written in clear and concise prose.

- The novel was praised for its eloquent prose and compelling storytelling.
- The professor assigned a challenging piece of prose for the students to analyze.

11. Plot
Synonyms: Storyline, Narrative, Sequence of events
Definition: The sequence of events that make up a story, including the exposition, rising action, climax, falling action, and resolution.
Examples:
- The plot of the novel was filled with unexpected twists and turns.
- The author skillfully developed the plot to keep readers engaged.
- The climax of the story was a pivotal moment that changed the course of events.
- The resolution neatly tied up all loose ends of the plot.
- The intricate plot left readers guessing until the very end.

12. Setting
Synonyms: Environment, Background, Time and place
Definition: The time and place in which a story takes place, including the physical, geographical, and cultural aspects.
Examples:
- The author vividly described the setting, transporting readers to a different time and place.
- The rural setting provided a serene backdrop for the unfolding events.
- The story was set in a bustling city during the 1920s.
- The desert setting added a sense of isolation and desolation to the narrative.
- The author carefully researched the historical setting to ensure accuracy.

13. Dialogue
Synonyms: Conversation, Discourse, Exchange

Definition: The conversation between characters in a literary work, often presented through direct quotations.

Examples:

- The dialogue between the two characters revealed their conflicting perspectives.

- The author's use of realistic dialogue brought the characters to life.

- The witty and humorous dialogue added levity to the story.

- The dialogue was filled with emotion, conveying the characters' inner thoughts and feelings.

- The playwright's skillful dialogue created intense dramatic moments on stage.

14. Metonymy

Synonyms: Figure of speech, Trope, Word substitution

Definition: A figure of speech in which a word or phrase is substituted for another closely associated word, often based on a specific relationship or attribute.

Examples:

- The pen is mightier than the sword. (Here, "pen" is a metonymy for writing and "sword" represents warfare.)

- The White House issued a statement. (Here, "White House" represents the U.S. government.)

- The crown represents the monarchy. (Here, "crown" is a metonymy for the monarchy and its power.)

- Hollywood is known for its glamour. (Here, "Hollywood" represents the film industry.)

- She has a love for the stage. (Here, "stage" represents theater and performing arts.)

15. Foil

Synonyms: Contrast, Counterpart, Opposite

Definition: A character who contrasts with another character, highlighting their differences and traits through comparison.

Examples:

- The protagonist and antagonist served as foils to each other, showcasing their opposing values.
- The gentle and kind-hearted protagonist had a villainous foil who represented evil.
- The foil character provided comic relief through their humorous and eccentric behavior.
- The protagonist's loyal friend acted as a foil, emphasizing the protagonist's courage and integrity.
- The foil character's cynicism and pessimism stood in stark contrast to the protagonist's optimism.

16. Motif

Synonyms: Symbol, Theme, Recurring element

Definition: A recurring image, idea, or symbol that contributes to the overall meaning and thematic development of a literary work.

Examples:
- The motif of the journey represented personal growth and transformation.
- The author used the motif of mirrors to explore the theme of self-reflection.
- The recurring motif of birds symbolized freedom and escape.
- The motif of light and darkness conveyed the duality of human nature.
- The motif of water was used to evoke a sense of purity and cleansing.

17. Allegory

Synonyms: Symbolism, Figurative representation, Extended metaphor

Definition: A story or narrative in which characters, settings, and events represent abstract ideas or moral qualities, often used to convey a deeper meaning or message.

Examples:
- The novel can be interpreted as an allegory for the human

struggle between good and evil.

- Animal Farm is an allegory that reflects political events and ideologies.

- The author's use of allegory allowed for social criticism in a fictional context.

- The allegorical tale conveyed a moral lesson about the consequences of greed.

- The story functioned as an allegory for the cycle of life and death.

18. Archetype

Synonyms: Prototype, Model, Exemplar

Definition: A typical character, symbol, or situation that represents a universal pattern, often recurring in literature and mythology.

Examples:

- The hero's journey is a common archetype found in various mythological and literary works.

- The wise old mentor archetype guided the protagonist on their quest.

- The damsel in distress archetype appears in many fairy tales and adventure stories.

- The trickster archetype adds a sense of mischief and unpredictability to the narrative.

- The archetype of the villain embodies evil and serves as the antagonist in the story.

19. Prose

Synonyms: Writing, Text, Composition

Definition: Written or spoken language in its ordinary form, without metrical structure, as distinguished from poetry.

Examples:

- The author's beautiful prose captivated the readers.

- She excelled in writing both poetry and prose.

- The essay was written in clear and concise prose.

- The novel was praised for its eloquent prose and compelling storytelling.

- The professor assigned a challenging piece of prose for the students to analyze.

20. Tone

Synonyms: Mood, Atmosphere, Attitude

Definition: The author's or narrator's attitude towards the subject matter or audience, conveyed through the choice of words, imagery, and style.

Examples:

- The author's tone in the passage was somber and melancholic.
- The tone of the poem shifted from joyful to mournful as it progressed.
- The novel's tone was humorous, filled with satire and wit.
- The author effectively created a suspenseful tone, keeping readers on edge.
- The play's tone was lighthearted and comedic, eliciting laughter from the audience.

14. Music

1. Melody
   Synonyms: Tune, Harmony, Air
   Definition: A sequence of musical notes that form a recognizable and memorable musical line.
   Examples:
   - The melody of the song is catchy and easily recognizable.
   - She hummed the beautiful melody as she walked down the street.
   - The violin played a haunting melody that touched the hearts of the audience.
   - The composer crafted a complex and intricate melody for the symphony.
   - The singer's voice soared with the melodic line of the ballad.

2. Rhythm
   Synonyms: Beat, Cadence, Pulse
   Definition: The pattern of regular or irregular beats in music that creates a sense of flow and movement.
   Examples:
   - The rhythm of the drums set the pace for the entire band.
   - She tapped her foot to the rhythm of the catchy song.
   - The dancers moved in perfect synchrony with the rhythm of the music.
   - The jazz band created a vibrant and energetic rhythm.
   - The composer experimented with different rhythmic patterns in the composition.

3. Harmony
   Synonyms: Chord, Concord, Accord
   Definition: The combination of simultaneous musical tones that create a pleasing and balanced sound.
   Examples:
   - The choir's harmonies added depth and richness to the performance.

- The guitarist strummed the chords in perfect harmony with the singer.
- The orchestra played a beautiful harmony that filled the concert hall.
- The vocal duet sang in exquisite harmony, their voices blending seamlessly.
- The pianist played the complex harmonies of the classical piece flawlessly.

4. Tempo
Synonyms: Speed, Pace, Rhythm
Definition: The speed at which a musical piece is performed or the rate of the underlying beat.
Examples:
- The conductor set a brisk tempo for the symphony.
- The song started slowly and gradually increased in tempo.
- The band played the lively tune at a fast tempo, energizing the crowd.
- The dancers moved gracefully to the slow tempo of the waltz.
- The drummer kept a steady tempo throughout the performance.

5. Instrument
Synonyms: Musical device, Tool, Apparatus
Definition: A device or object used to produce musical sounds, typically played by a musician.
Examples:
- The violin is a versatile and expressive instrument.
- He is skilled at playing multiple instruments, including the piano and guitar.
- The orchestra consisted of various instruments, including brass, strings, and woodwinds.
- She carefully tuned her instrument before the recital.
- The drummer showcased his mastery of the percussion instruments.

6. Composition

Synonyms: Musical piece, Work, Creation

Definition: A piece of music that has been created or written, often consisting of multiple sections or movements.

Examples:

- The composer's latest composition was received with critical acclaim.

- He spent hours composing the symphony, carefully crafting each section.

- The pianist performed a beautiful composition by a renowned composer.

- She is known for her innovative compositions that blend different musical genres.

- The orchestra rehearsed the complex composition in preparation for the concert.

7. Genre

Synonyms: Style, Category, Type

Definition: A category or classification of music based on its characteristics, style, or historical period.

Examples:

- Jazz is a genre known for its improvisation and syncopated rhythms.

- She enjoys listening to various genres of music, including pop, rock, and classical.

- The band's music falls into the alternative rock genre.

- The composer experimented with blending different genres in his latest album.

- The orchestra performed a program featuring music from different genres.

8. Concert

Synonyms: Performance, Show, Gig

Definition: A public musical performance given by one or more musicians or bands.

Examples:

- The band played a sold-out concert at the stadium.

- She attended a classical concert at the renowned music hall.
- The guitarist gave an electrifying solo during the concert.
- The symphony orchestra performed a memorable concert for the audience.
- The singer's concert showcased her incredible vocal range and stage presence.

9. Solo

Synonyms: Individual performance, Unaccompanied, Alone

Definition: A musical performance or passage performed by a single musician without accompaniment.

Examples:

- The pianist played a mesmerizing solo during the concert.
- He performed a beautiful guitar solo that showcased his technical skill.
- The flutist played a hauntingly beautiful solo piece.
- The violinist's solo performance captivated the audience.
- The singer's powerful voice filled the room during her solo.

10. Orchestra

Synonyms: Symphony, Ensemble, Philharmonic

Definition: A large group of musicians playing various instruments together, often led by a conductor.

Examples:

- The orchestra rehearsed for hours before the performance.
- The symphony orchestra performed a classical masterpiece.
- The conductor led the orchestra with precision and passion.
- The orchestra's performance was met with a standing ovation.
- The talented musicians joined the community orchestra.

11. Chorus

Synonyms: Choir, Ensemble, Vocal group

Definition: A group of singers performing together, often providing the background vocals or harmonies.

Examples:

- The chorus sang in perfect harmony, adding depth to the

song.

- She joined the school chorus to showcase her singing talent.
- The choir performed a breathtaking chorus that moved the audience.
- The chorus line danced and sang with energy and enthusiasm.
- The musical featured a memorable chorus number.

12. Lyrics

Synonyms: Words, Songtext, Verses

Definition: The words or text of a song, typically expressing emotions, thoughts, or storytelling.

Examples:
- She wrote heartfelt lyrics for her latest song.
- The singer's powerful voice brought the lyrics to life.
- The audience sang along to the familiar lyrics of the popular song.
- The songwriter penned poetic and meaningful lyrics.
- The ballad's lyrics conveyed a tale of love and loss.

13. Harmony

Synonyms: Accord, Consistency, Congruity

Definition: The pleasing combination of musical tones played or sung simultaneously, creating a sense of unity and balance.

Examples:
- The choir's harmonies blended beautifully, creating a rich and full sound.
- The guitar and piano played in harmony, complementing each other's melodies.
- The band members practiced diligently to achieve perfect harmony in their performance.
- The vocal group harmonized flawlessly, producing a captivating and mesmerizing sound.
- The orchestra's harmonies resonated throughout the concert hall, captivating the audience.

14. Crescendo

Synonyms: Increase, Build-up, Intensification
Definition: A gradual increase in volume, intensity, or force in a musical piece.
Examples:
- The music swelled with a gradual crescendo, building up to a climactic moment.
- The conductor signaled the orchestra to play with a crescendo, gradually growing louder.
- The pianist's fingers danced across the keys, creating a beautiful crescendo of sound.
- The band created

a dramatic crescendo, capturing the audience's attention.
- The singer's voice rose with a powerful crescendo, leaving the audience in awe.

15. Decrescendo
Synonyms: Decrease, Diminuendo, Subside
Definition: A gradual decrease in volume, intensity, or force in a musical piece.
Examples:
- The music softened with a decrescendo, gently fading away.
- The conductor guided the orchestra to play with a decrescendo, gradually becoming quieter.
- The guitarist strummed the final chords with a decrescendo, ending the song softly.
- The band concluded the performance with a beautiful decrescendo, leaving the audience in silence.
- The singer's voice diminished with a delicate decrescendo, creating a serene atmosphere.

16. Improvisation
Synonyms: Spontaneity, Ad-lib, Unplanned
Definition: Creating or performing music spontaneously without prior preparation or scripted notation.
Examples:
- The jazz musician showcased his improvisation skills

during the solo section.

- The guitarist amazed the audience with his incredible improvisation on stage.

- The pianist added a touch of improvisation to the classical piece, showcasing her creativity.

- The band members engaged in a lively improvisation session, creating unique musical moments.

- The singer's ability to improvise lyrics on the spot impressed the audience.

17. Vibrato

Synonyms: Tremolo, Quaver, Trill

Definition: A slight variation in pitch, producing a vibrant and expressive tone, typically applied to sustained notes.

Examples:

- The violinist played the beautiful melody with a delicate vibrato, adding emotional depth to the music.

- The singer's voice quivered with a controlled vibrato, enhancing the dramatic effect of the song.

- The cellist's skilled use of vibrato created a rich and resonant sound.

- The saxophonist applied a subtle vibrato to the long notes, giving them a warm and expressive quality.

- The vocalist demonstrated her versatility by using vibrato in different musical genres.

18. Overture

Synonyms: Prelude, Introduction, Prologue

Definition: An orchestral piece or musical introduction that sets the tone or theme for a larger musical work, such as an opera or musical.

Examples:

- The orchestra performed the grand overture, setting the stage for the opera.

- The overture captivated the audience, providing a glimpse of the musical journey to come.

- The composer composed a beautiful and evocative overture for the symphony.
- The musical started with an energetic and lively overture, instantly grabbing the audience's attention.
- The conductor led the orchestra through the dynamic overture, creating a sense of anticipation.

19. Duet
   Synonyms: Pair, Duo, Partnership
   Definition: A musical performance or composition featuring two performers, often singing or playing instruments together.
   Examples:
   - The vocal duet performed a heartfelt love song, their voices blending in perfect harmony.
   - The pianist and violinist played a captivating duet, showcasing their musical synergy.
   - The band members collaborated on a beautiful duet, exchanging melodic phrases.
   - The singers shared the stage for a powerful duet, their voices complementing each other.
   - The guitarist and drummer performed an energetic duet, creating a rhythmic and melodic interplay.

20. Encore
   Synonyms: Repeat, Extra, Additional performance
   Definition: An additional performance or request for an additional performance in response to an enthusiastic audience.
   Examples:
   - The crowd cheered and clapped, demanding an encore from the band.
   - The singer returned to the stage for an encore, performing a fan-favorite song.
   - The orchestra delighted the audience with an encore, playing a lively and upbeat piece.
   - The pianist received a standing ovation and came back for an encore, performing a breathtaking solo.

- The band ended the concert with an encore, leaving the audience wanting more.

15. Fashion and Style

1. Trend
   Synonyms: Fashion, Style, Craze
   Definition: A popular or fashionable way of dressing, behaving, or doing something.
   Examples:
   - High-waisted jeans are currently a trend among young people.
   - Animal prints have made a comeback as a fashion trend this season.
   - The latest trend in footwear is chunky sneakers.
   - She always keeps up with the latest fashion trends.
   - This year, pastel colors are trending in the fashion industry.

2. Couture
   Synonyms: High fashion, Designer fashion, Haute couture
   Definition: High-quality, custom-made clothing created by fashion designers.
   Examples:
   - The fashion show featured stunning couture designs.
   - The actress wore a beautiful couture gown on the red carpet.
   - Only a few people can afford to buy couture clothing.
   - The fashion designer is renowned for his couture creations.
   - She dreams of wearing a couture dress on her wedding day.

3. Accessory
   Synonyms: Ornament, Adornment, Accent
   Definition: A supplementary item that adds to or complements someone's outfit, such as jewelry, handbags, or scarves.
   Examples:
   - She loves to wear colorful accessories to enhance her outfits.
   - The necklace is the perfect accessory to complete her look.
   - He always carries a stylish briefcase as his go-to accessory.
   - A hat can be both a fashionable and functional accessory.

- The fashion boutique sells a wide range of accessories, including belts and sunglasses.

4. Vintage

Synonyms: Retro, Classic, Antique

Definition: Clothing or accessories that are from a previous era or period, typically considered stylish and of high quality.

Examples:

- She found a beautiful vintage dress at the thrift store.
- The actress wore a vintage fur coat to the award ceremony.
- Vintage-inspired fashion is gaining popularity among young people.
- He collects vintage watches as a hobby.
- The fashion designer drew inspiration from vintage fashion trends.

5. Designer

Synonyms: Fashion designer, Couturier, Stylist

Definition: A person who creates or designs fashionable clothing or accessories.

Examples:

- She aspires to become a famous fashion designer one day.
- The designer showcased her latest collection at the fashion show.
- Many celebrities wear dresses designed by famous fashion designers.
- The boutique sells a range of designer labels.
- The designer's creations are known for their unique and innovative designs.

6. Stylish

Synonyms: Fashionable, Trendy, Chic

Definition: Having a smart, fashionable, or elegant appearance.

Examples:

- She always looks stylish no matter the occasion.
- He has a great sense of style and dresses in a stylish way.

- The fashion magazine provides tips on how to dress stylishly.
- The new collection offers stylish options for both casual and formal wear.
- The designer's outfits are known for their stylish and modern designs.

7. Runway

Synonyms: Catwalk, Fashion show, Ramp

Definition: A long platform used for models to showcase clothing during a fashion show.

Examples:

- The fashion models strutted down the runway with confidence.
- The designer presented his latest collection on the runway.
- The fashion show featured stunning designs on the runway.
- The audience eagerly awaited the models' appearances on the runway.
- She dreams of walking the runway at a prestigious fashion event.

8. Haute couture

Synonyms: High fashion, Designer fashion, Couture

Definition: Exclusive, custom-made clothing created by high-end fashion houses.

Examples:

- The fashion week showcased the best of haute couture.
- Haute couture dresses are meticulously crafted and highly sought after.
- The designer specializes in haute couture bridal gowns.
- The celebrities were dressed in stunning haute couture outfits for the event.
- She aspires to work in the world of haute couture as a fashion designer.

9. Tailor

Synonyms: Seamstress, Dressmaker, Fitter

Definition: A person who makes, alters, or repairs clothing to fit an individual's body shape and measurements.

Examples:

- She took her dress to a tailor to have it altered.
- The tailor crafted a custom suit for the groom.
- The boutique offers tailor-made services for personalized clothing.
- The tailor is known for their excellent craftsmanship and attention to detail.
- He learned how to sew from his grandmother, who was a skilled tailor.

10. Fashionable

Synonyms: Stylish, Trendy, In vogue

Definition: Being in current fashion or style; following or setting trends.

Examples:

- She always stays updated with the latest fashion trends.
- The fashion designer is known for creating fashionable and innovative designs.
- The store offers a wide range of fashionable clothing for all ages.
- The fashion magazine provides tips on how to stay fashionable on a budget.
- He likes to experiment with different styles to create his own fashionable look.

11. Boutique

Synonyms: Fashion store, Clothing store, Fashion shop

Definition: A small shop that specializes in fashionable clothing, accessories, or specialty items.

Examples:

- She found a unique dress at a trendy boutique in the city.
- The boutique offers a curated collection of designer clothing.
- Many boutique owners travel to find unique fashion pieces for their store.

- The boutique's window display showcases the latest fashion trends.
- She enjoys supporting local boutiques to find one-of-a-kind pieces.

12. Ensemble
Synonyms: Outfit, Attire, Costume
Definition: A coordinated set of clothing items worn together to create a stylish or complete look.
Examples:
- She put together a fashionable ensemble for the evening event.
- The actress wore a stunning ensemble on the red carpet.
- The fashion blogger shared tips on how to create a stylish ensemble.
- His ensemble consisted of a tailored suit and a matching tie.
- The fashion magazine featured different ensembles for various occasions.

13. Accessories
Synonyms: Add-ons, Embellishments, Trimmings
Definition: Supplementary items that enhance or complete an outfit, such as jewelry, belts, scarves, or hats.
Examples:
- She loves to experiment with different accessories to elevate her outfits.
- The bracelet and necklace are beautiful accessories that complement her dress.
- A well-chosen accessory can transform a simple outfit into a stylish ensemble.
- The store offers a wide range of accessories, including handbags and sunglasses.
- He always carries a stylish accessory, such as a pocket square, to add a touch of sophistication.

14. Couturier
Synonyms: Fashion designer, Dressmaker, Tailor

Definition: A person or designer who creates custom-made, high-fashion clothing.

Examples:

- The couturier presented a collection of exquisite gowns at the fashion show.

- Many celebrities prefer to work with renowned couturiers for their red carpet looks.

- The fashion house is known for its talented couturiers and their attention to detail.

- The couturier specializes in creating one-of-a-kind wedding dresses.

- She dreams of becoming a successful couturier and showcasing her designs on the runway.

15. Runway

Synonyms: Catwalk, Ramp, Fashion show

Definition: A narrow platform or stage where models walk to showcase clothing during a fashion show.

Examples:

- The models confidently strutted down the runway, showcasing the designer's collection.

- The fashion week featured multiple runway shows displaying the latest trends.

- The designer chose a unique runway setup for their fashion presentation.

- The audience eagerly watched as the models made their way down the runway.

- She aspires to walk the runway and fulfill her dream of becoming a fashion model.

16. Designer

Synonyms: Fashion designer, Couturier, Stylist

Definition: A person who creates or designs fashionable clothing or accessories.

Examples:

- The renowned designer showcased their latest collection at the fashion event.

- Many celebrities wear outfits designed by famous fashion designers.

- The fashion industry is highly competitive, with many aspiring designers.

- The designer's creations are known for their unique and innovative designs.

- She admires the work of several influential fashion designers.

17. Stylish

Synonyms: Fashionable, Trendy, Chic

Definition: Having a smart, fashionable, or elegant appearance.

Examples:

- She always dresses stylishly and is admired for her fashion sense.

- The stylish couple turned heads as they entered the event.

- The fashion magazine provides tips on how to create stylish looks.

- The new collection offers stylish options for both casual and formal wear.

- The actress is known for her stylish red carpet outfits.

18. Elegance

Synonyms: Grace, Refinement, Sophistication

Definition: Graceful and stylish in appearance or manner; characterized by good taste and class.

Examples:

- The evening gown exuded elegance and sophistication.

- She carries herself with elegance and poise in any situation.

- The designer's creations are known for their timeless elegance.

- The fashion show featured a collection of elegant and refined pieces.

- The actress was praised for her elegance and beauty on the red carpet.

19. Runway

Synonyms: Catwalk, Fashion show, Ramp

Definition: A long platform used for models to showcase clothing during a fashion show.

Examples:

- The fashion models confidently walked down the runway.

- The designer's latest collection was showcased on the runway.

- The audience eagerly awaited the models' appearances on the runway.

- The fashion show featured stunning designs on the runway.

- She dreams of walking the runway at a prestigious fashion event.

20. Accessory

Synonyms: Ornament, Adornment, Accent

Definition: An additional item that complements or enhances someone's outfit, such as jewelry, handbags, or scarves.

Examples:

- She loves to accessorize her outfits with statement necklaces.

- The clutch bag is the perfect accessory to complete her evening look.

- A well-chosen accessory can elevate a simple outfit.

- The store offers a wide range of accessories, including belts and hats.

- He always wears a stylish accessory, like a pocket square, to add a touch of flair.

16. Philosophy and Ethics

1. Morality
   Synonyms: Ethics, Virtue, Righteousness
   Definition: Principles or rules of right conduct, involving distinctions between right and wrong behaviour.
   Examples:
   - The philosopher discussed the concept of morality in his lecture.
   - Personal morality shapes one's ethical decisions and actions.
   - The society's morality is reflected in its laws and social norms.
   - He faced a moral dilemma and had to make a difficult choice.
   - The book explores the complexities of morality in different cultural contexts.

2. Objectivity
   Synonyms: Impartiality, Neutrality, Fairness
   Definition: The quality of being unbiased, neutral, or based on factual evidence rather than personal feelings or opinions.
   Examples:
   - The journalist strived for objectivity in reporting the news.
   - The philosopher argued that achieving complete objectivity is challenging due to inherent biases.
   - The scientific study was conducted with strict objectivity to ensure reliable results.
   - Objectivity is essential in evaluating evidence and making informed judgments.
   - The judge maintained objectivity throughout the trial proceedings.

3. Rationality
   Synonyms: Reason, Logic, Soundness
   Definition: The quality of being based on or in accordance with reason or logic.
   Examples:

- The philosopher emphasized the importance of rationality in decision-making.
- The argument presented was not grounded in rationality or evidence.
- The scientific method relies on rationality and empirical evidence.
- Rationality is a fundamental aspect of critical thinking.
- The rationality of his actions was questioned by the jury.

4. Metaphysics

Synonyms: Ontology, Existence, Reality

Definition: The branch of philosophy that deals with the fundamental nature of reality and existence.

Examples:

- The philosopher delved into the realm of metaphysics to explore the nature of being.
- Questions about the existence of God fall within the domain of metaphysics.
- The concept of time is often discussed in metaphysics.
- Metaphysics explores the nature of consciousness and its relation to the physical world.
- The philosopher proposed a new metaphysical theory on the nature of reality.

5. Epistemology

Synonyms: Knowledge theory, Theory of knowledge, Cognitive science

Definition: The branch of philosophy that examines the nature of knowledge, belief, and justification.

Examples:

- Epistemology explores how we acquire knowledge and what constitutes reliable knowledge.
- The philosopher questioned the reliability of sensory perception in epistemology.
- Epistemological debates revolve around the sources and limits of knowledge.

- The study of epistemology is essential in understanding the foundations of science.
- The philosopher proposed a new epistemological framework based on empirical evidence.

6. Existentialism

Synonyms: Existence philosophy, Humanism, Individualism

Definition: A philosophical movement emphasizing individual existence, freedom, and responsibility.

Examples:

- The existentialist philosopher explored the meaning of life and the freedom of choice.
- Existentialism emphasizes the importance of individual authenticity and self-determination.
- The protagonist in the novel grapples with existentialist questions of existence and purpose.
- Existentialist thinkers reject the idea of predetermined destiny.
- The philosopher's work influenced the development of existentialist thought.

7. Utilitarianism

Synonyms: Consequentialism, Pragmatism, Maximization

Definition: A moral theory that holds actions should be judged by their overall utility or benefit to the majority.

Examples:

- Utilitarianism considers the greatest happiness for the greatest number of people as the guiding principle.
- The ethical dilemma was approached from a utilitarian perspective.
- The utilitarian approach to decision-making prioritizes the collective well-being.
- Critics argue that utilitarianism overlooks individual rights and justice.
- The philosopher defended the principles of utilitarianism in his essay.

8. Hedonism

Synonyms: Pleasure-seeking, Epicureanism, Sensualism

Definition: The pursuit of pleasure or the doctrine that pleasure is the highest good.

Examples:

- Hedonism suggests that maximizing pleasure is the ultimate goal in life.

- The protagonist's hedonistic lifestyle led to self-destructive behavior.

- Critics argue that hedonism overlooks the importance of moral responsibility.

- The philosopher debated the merits of hedonism versus other ethical theories.

- Hedonistic tendencies can lead to short-term gratification but may have long-term consequences.

9. Syllogism

Synonyms: Logical argument, Deductive reasoning, Inference

Definition: A form of deductive reasoning consisting of a major premise, a minor premise, and a conclusion.

Examples:

- Syllogism is a foundational tool in logical reasoning.

- The philosopher presented a compelling syllogism to support his argument.

- The teacher explained how to construct a valid syllogism in the logic class.

- The detective used syllogistic reasoning to solve the crime.

- Understanding syllogism helps in critically analyzing arguments.

10. Empiricism

Synonyms: Observation, Experimentation, Evidence-based

Definition: The theory that knowledge comes primarily from sensory experience and empirical evidence.

Examples:

- Empiricism emphasizes the importance of observation and

evidence in acquiring knowledge.

- The scientist conducted experiments to gather empirical data supporting the theory.
- The philosopher critiqued the limitations of pure empiricism in understanding complex concepts.
- Empiricism forms the foundation of the scientific method.
- The researcher's findings were based on a rigorous empirical study.

11. Aesthetics

Synonyms: Beauty, Artistry, Taste

Definition: The philosophical study of beauty, art, and the nature of aesthetic experiences.

Examples:

- Aesthetics explores the subjective perception of beauty in art and nature.
- The art critic analyzed the aesthetics of the painting, focusing on color and composition.
- The philosopher discussed the relationship between aesthetics and ethics in art.
- The museum curator carefully curated the exhibition to highlight the aesthetics of each piece.
- She has a deep appreciation for the aesthetics of architecture and design.

12. Ethics

Synonyms: Morality, Principles, Morals

Definition: Moral principles that govern a person's behavior or the conduct of an activity.

Examples:

- The company has a strong code of ethics that employees must adhere to.
- Medical professionals are expected to follow ethical guidelines in their practice.
- The ethics of animal testing are a subject of ongoing debate.
- Business ethics play a crucial role in maintaining trust with

customers.

- The ethics of technology use raise important ethical questions.

13. Subjectivity

Synonyms: Personal perspective, Individual experience, Bias

Definition: The quality of being based on personal feelings, opinions, or interpretations rather than objective facts.

Examples:

- The art critic acknowledged the subjectivity of their interpretation of the painting.
- The philosopher explored the limitations of subjectivity in understanding reality.
- Different people may have different subjective experiences of the same event.
- Subjectivity influences one's perception and response to works of literature.
- The discussion touched upon the subjective nature of beauty and taste.

14. Teleology

Synonyms: Purpose, Finality, Goal-oriented

Definition: The study of ends, purposes, or goals in natural phenomena or human behavior.

Examples:

- Teleology examines the purpose or end result of actions or events.
- The philosopher argued that teleology plays a role in shaping human behavior.
- The concept of teleology is central to understanding evolutionary biology.
- The debate explored whether human history follows a teleological progression.
- The architect designed the building with a teleological approach, prioritizing functionality and user experience.

15. Nihilism

Synonyms: Anarchy, Negation, Rejection

Definition: The belief that life is without objective meaning, value, or purpose.

Examples:

- Nihilism posits that life lacks inherent meaning or purpose.

- The protagonist in the novel embraced a nihilistic worldview.

- The philosopher criticized nihilism as an intellectually unsatisfying position.

- Nihilism challenges traditional moral and religious frameworks.

- The artist's work often explores existential themes and nihilistic tendencies.

16. Pragmatism

Synonyms: Practicality, Realism, Utilitarianism

Definition: A philosophical approach that focuses on practical consequences and the usefulness of ideas or actions.

Examples:

- Pragmatism emphasizes the importance of practicality and real-world application.

- The philosopher advocated for a pragmatic approach to problem-solving.

- Pragmatism rejects abstract theories that have no practical implications.

- The politician's decisions were driven by pragmatism rather than ideology.

- Pragmatic thinking helps in finding practical solutions to complex problems.

17. Idealism

Synonyms: Vision, Optimism, Utopianism

Definition: The belief in or pursuit of ideals, principles, or perfection.

Examples:

- Idealism envisions a better world based on noble principles and values.

- The philosopher proposed an idealistic vision of a just society.

- Idealism often clashes with the constraints of practical reality.

- The artist's work is inspired by the ideals of beauty and harmony.

- The idealism of youth gives way to a more realistic worldview over time.

18. Dialectic

Synonyms: Dialogue, Debate, Argumentation

Definition: The art of investigating or discussing the truth of opinions, typically through logical reasoning and argumentation.

Examples:

- Dialectic involves a process of reasoned dialogue to arrive at the truth or resolution of conflicting ideas.

- The philosopher engaged in a dialectic with his peers to refine his theories.

- The dialectic method encourages critical thinking and intellectual exploration.

- The debate team employed dialectic techniques to present persuasive arguments.

- Dialectical reasoning helps in understanding and resolving conflicting viewpoints.

19. Humanism

Synonyms: Human-centered, Compassion, Altruism

Definition: A philosophical and ethical stance that emphasizes the value, dignity, and potential of human beings.

Examples:

- Humanism emphasizes the importance of human well-being, happiness, and fulfillment.

- The philosopher advocated for a humanistic approach to education, focusing on individual growth.

- Humanism celebrates human achievements in science, art, and culture.
- The humanistic perspective places human needs and values at the center of ethical decision-making.
- The organization works towards social justice and humanistic principles.

20. Relativism

Synonyms: Subjectivity, Pluralism, Cultural diversity

Definition: The belief that truth, morality, and knowledge are not absolute but are relative to individuals, cultures, or historical contexts.

Examples:
- Relativism asserts that truth and morality are subjective and vary across different cultures.
- The philosopher challenged the notion of objective truth and advocated for relativism.
- Relativism acknowledges the influence of cultural norms on moral judgments.
- The concept of relativism raises questions about the universality of ethical principles.
- Relativism challenges the idea of a single, objective interpretation of reality.

17. Psychology

1. Cognitive
   Synonyms: Mental, Intellectual, Cognitive-behavioral
   Definition: Relating to the processes of thought, perception, and understanding.
   Examples:
   - Cognitive development refers to the growth of intellectual abilities in individuals.
   - The psychologist specializes in cognitive therapy for treating anxiety disorders.
   - The study investigated the cognitive effects of sleep deprivation on memory.
   - Cognitive neuroscience explores the neural mechanisms underlying cognitive processes.
   - The child's cognitive skills improved through educational interventions.

2. Perception
   Synonyms: Awareness, Sensation, Consciousness
   Definition: The process of recognizing, interpreting, and giving meaning to sensory information.
   Examples:
   - Perception plays a crucial role in shaping our understanding of the world.
   - The psychologist studied visual perception and how it influences decision-making.
   - The experiment examined the effect of priming on participants' perception of colors.
   - Cultural factors can influence individuals' perception of beauty and attractiveness.
   - The artist's work challenges traditional perceptions of reality.

3. Behavior
   Synonyms: Conduct, Actions, Mannerisms

Definition: Observable actions, reactions, or conduct of an individual or organism.

Examples:

- The psychologist analyzed the behavior of participants in a social experiment.

- Environmental factors can influence behavior, shaping one's responses to stimuli.

- The study explored the relationship between genetics and aggressive behavior.

- Positive reinforcement can be an effective way to modify behavior.

- The therapist used behavior therapy techniques to address maladaptive behaviors.

4. Motivation

Synonyms: Drive, Incentive, Ambition

Definition: The internal or external factors that drive an individual to act or behave in a certain way.

Examples:

- Motivation is essential for achieving goals and success.

- The psychologist studied the role of intrinsic motivation in enhancing performance.

- Monetary rewards can serve as extrinsic motivation for employees.

- Lack of motivation can hinder progress and lead to procrastination.

- The athlete's strong motivation and determination propelled her to win the race.

5. Personality

Synonyms: Character, Disposition, Temperament

Definition: The unique pattern of thoughts, feelings, and behaviors that define an individual.

Examples:

- Personality traits such as extroversion and agreeableness impact social interactions.

- The psychologist assessed the client's personality through various psychological tests.
- The study explored the relationship between personality and job satisfaction.
- The artist's work reflects her distinct personality and artistic style.
- Personality disorders can significantly affect an individual's daily functioning.

6. Emotion
Synonyms: Feeling, Sentiment, Affect
Definition: A complex psychological state involving subjective experiences, physiological changes, and expressive behaviors.
Examples:
- Emotions play a crucial role in human experience and interpersonal relationships.
- The psychologist studied the effects of emotions on decision-making processes.
- The film evoked strong emotions of joy and sadness in the audience.
- Emotional intelligence refers to the ability to recognize and manage one's own emotions.
- Traumatic experiences can lead to long-lasting emotional disturbances.

7. Stress
Synonyms: Pressure, Tension, Strain
Definition: A physiological or psychological response to demanding or challenging situations.
Examples:
- Chronic stress can have detrimental effects on physical and mental health.
- The psychologist provided stress management techniques to help clients cope with anxiety.
- The study examined the impact of stress on cognitive functioning.

- Job-related stress can lead to burnout and decreased productivity.
- The relaxation techniques helped reduce the participant's stress levels.

8. Memory
Synonyms: Recall, Retention, Remembrance
Definition: The cognitive process of encoding, storing, and retrieving information.
Examples:
- Memory allows us to retain and recall past experiences and knowledge.
- The psychologist conducted research on the role of memory in eyewitness testimony.
- The study investigated the effects of sleep on memory consolidation.
- Alzheimer's disease is characterized by progressive memory loss.
- The student used mnemonic devices to improve memory recall during exams.

9. Development
Synonyms: Growth, Progress, Advancement
Definition: The process of progressive and sequential changes in physical, cognitive, and socio-emotional domains over time.
Examples:
- Child development refers to the changes in physical and cognitive abilities as children grow.
- The psychologist studied the socio-emotional development of adolescents.
- The study examined the effects of early experiences on brain development.
- Lifespan development encompasses the changes that occur from birth to old age.
- The therapy program focused on promoting healthy development in children.

10. Intelligence

Synonyms: Intellectual, Smartness, Aptitude

Definition: The ability to acquire and apply knowledge, problem-solving skills, and adapt to new situations.

Examples:

- Intelligence is a multifaceted construct that encompasses various cognitive abilities.

- The psychologist assessed the participant's IQ to measure intellectual functioning.

- Emotional intelligence involves understanding and managing one's own emotions and others'.

- The study explored the relationship between creativity and intelligence.

- The child's exceptional intelligence was evident from an early age.

11. Consciousness

Synonyms: Awareness, Wakefulness, Mindfulness

Definition: The state of being aware of one's thoughts, emotions, and surroundings.

Examples:

- Consciousness is a fundamental aspect of human experience.

- The psychologist investigated altered states of consciousness during meditation.

- The study explored the neural correlates of conscious awareness.

- The accident caused a temporary loss of consciousness in the victim.

- Mindfulness practices aim to cultivate present-moment awareness and consciousness.

12. Perception

Synonyms: Awareness, Sensation, Consciousness

Definition: The process of recognizing, interpreting, and giving meaning to sensory information.

Examples:
- Perception plays a crucial role in shaping our understanding of the world.
- The psychologist studied visual perception and how it influences decision-making.
- The experiment examined the effect of priming on participants' perception of colors.
- Cultural factors can influence individuals' perception of beauty and attractiveness.
- The artist's work challenges traditional perceptions of reality.

13. Behaviorism

Synonyms: Conditioning, Learning, Operant behavior

Definition: A psychological approach that focuses on observable behavior and the principles of conditioning.

Examples:
- Behaviorism emphasizes the role of environmental factors in shaping behavior.
- The psychologist used behaviorist principles to modify the client's maladaptive behaviors.
- Classical conditioning is a fundamental concept in behaviorism.
- The study investigated the effects of positive reinforcement on behavior change.
- The behaviorist perspective downplays the influence of internal mental processes.

14. Psychopathology

Synonyms: Mental illness, Abnormal psychology, Psychiatric disorder

Definition: The study of mental disorders or abnormal behaviors and the factors that contribute to their development.

Examples:
- Psychopathology seeks to understand the causes and symptoms of psychological disorders.

- The psychologist specialized in diagnosing and treating psychopathology.
- The study examined the prevalence of psychopathology in different populations.
- The patient's symptoms were indicative of a specific psychopathological condition.
- The field of psychopathology has made significant advancements in understanding mental illness.

15. Therapy
Synonyms: Treatment, Counseling, Intervention
Definition: The process of providing professional assistance and support to individuals experiencing psychological difficulties.
Examples:
- Therapy can help individuals cope with and overcome various mental health challenges.
- The psychologist employed cognitive-behavioral therapy to treat the client's anxiety.
- Family therapy focuses on improving communication and resolving conflicts within a family system.
- The study evaluated the efficacy of different therapy modalities for depression.
- The therapist provided ongoing support and guidance throughout the therapeutic process.

16. Psychologist
Synonyms: Mental health professional, Psychotherapist, Counselor
Definition: A trained professional who studies human behavior, cognition, and emotions and provides psychological services.
Examples:
- The psychologist conducted research on memory and cognition.

- The clinical psychologist specializes in diagnosing and treating mental health disorders.
- The school psychologist provides counseling and support to students.
- The study recruited participants from diverse backgrounds to ensure generalizability.
- The psychologist's role is to help individuals improve their psychological well-being.

17. Perception
   Synonyms: Awareness, Sensation, Consciousness
   Definition: The process of recognizing, interpreting, and giving meaning to sensory information.
   Examples:
   - Perception plays a crucial role in shaping our understanding of the world.
   - The psychologist studied visual perception and how it influences decision-making.
   - The experiment examined the effect of priming on participants' perception of colors.
   - Cultural factors can influence individuals' perception of beauty and attractiveness.
   - The artist's work challenges traditional perceptions of reality.

18. Abnormality
   Synonyms: Anomaly, Deviation, Irregularity
   Definition: Departure from what is considered typical, normal, or expected in behavior, thoughts, or emotions.
   Examples:
   - The psychologist assessed the client's symptoms to determine the presence of abnormality.
   - The study investigated the prevalence of abnormality in a specific population.
   - Abnormal psychology focuses on understanding and treating psychological disorders.

- The patient's behavior exhibited clear signs of abnormality.
- The therapist used a standardized assessment to measure the degree of abnormality.

19. Perception
Synonyms: Awareness, Sensation, Consciousness
Definition: The process of recognizing, interpreting, and giving meaning to sensory information.
Examples:
- Perception plays a crucial role in shaping our understanding of the world.
- The psychologist studied visual perception and how it influences decision-making.
- The experiment examined the effect of priming on participants' perception of colors.
- Cultural factors can influence individuals' perception of beauty and attractiveness.
- The artist's work challenges traditional perceptions of reality.

20. Resilience
Synonyms: Adaptability, Endurance, Tenacity
Definition: The ability to bounce back, recover, and cope with adversity, stress, or challenges.
Examples:
- Resilience is a key factor in maintaining psychological well-being.
- The psychologist focused on fostering resilience in individuals who experienced trauma.
- The study examined the protective factors that contribute to resilience in children.
- The individual's resilience allowed them to overcome difficult life circumstances.
- Resilience can be cultivated through social support, positive coping strategies, and self-care.

21. Intelligence

Synonyms: Intellectual, Smartness, Aptitude

Definition: The ability to acquire and apply knowledge, problem-solving skills, and adapt to new situations.

Examples:

- Intelligence is a multifaceted construct that encompasses various cognitive abilities.

- The psychologist assessed the participant's IQ to measure intellectual functioning.

- Emotional intelligence involves understanding and managing one's own emotions and others'.

- The

study explored the relationship between creativity and intelligence.

- The child's exceptional intelligence was evident from an early age.

22. Conditioning

Synonyms: Training, Learning, Indoctrination

Definition: The process of learning associations between stimuli and responses through repeated exposure and reinforcement.

Examples:

- Classical conditioning is a foundational concept in psychology.

- The psychologist used operant conditioning techniques to modify the patient's behavior.

- The study investigated the effects of conditioning on the formation of habits.

- The experiment demonstrated how conditioning can influence decision-making.

- Parenting practices can inadvertently reinforce certain conditioning patterns in children.

23. Psychosocial

Synonyms: Socioemotional, Behavioral, Psychological

Definition: Relating to the interaction between psychological processes and social factors.

Examples:

- The psychologist studied the psychosocial factors contributing to addiction.

- The study explored the impact of psychosocial stressors on mental health outcomes.

- The therapist provided psychosocial support to help the client navigate relationship issues.

- The psychosocial development of children is influenced by familial and societal factors.

- The research highlighted the importance of addressing both psychological and social aspects of well-being.

24. Empathy

Synonyms: Compassion, Understanding, Sensitivity

Definition: The ability to understand and share the feelings and experiences of another person.

Examples:

- Empathy is essential for building meaningful connections and fostering compassion.

- The psychologist emphasized the importance of empathy in therapeutic relationships.

- The study investigated the relationship between empathy and prosocial behavior.

- The teacher showed empathy towards the student struggling with personal challenges.

- The novel evoked empathy in readers by depicting the protagonist's emotional journey.

25. Consciousness

Synonyms: Awareness, Wakefulness, Mindfulness

Definition: The state of being aware of one's thoughts, emotions, and surroundings.

Examples:

- Consciousness is a fundamental aspect of human experience.

- The psychologist investigated altered states of consciousness during meditation.
- The study explored the neural correlates of conscious awareness.
- The accident caused a temporary loss of consciousness in the victim.
- Mindfulness practices aim to cultivate present-moment awareness and consciousness.

18. Religion and Spirituality

1. Belief
Synonyms: Faith, Conviction, Trust
Definition: A strong mental acceptance or trust in something, often based on religious or spiritual teachings.
Examples:
- His belief in the afterlife gave him comfort during times of grief.
- The community shares a common belief in the power of prayer.
- She holds a strong belief in the existence of a higher power.
- The speaker emphasized the importance of respecting different religious beliefs.
- My personal belief is that kindness and compassion should guide our actions.

2. Worship
Synonyms: Adoration, Devotion, Reverence
Definition: Showing reverence, honor, and respect to a deity or higher power through religious rituals and practices.
Examples:
- The community gathers every Sunday to worship at the local church.
- Muslims around the world participate in daily prayers as a form of worship.
- She finds solace and connection through her personal worship practices.
- The ceremony involved singing hymns and offering prayers as an act of worship.
- Many cultures have unique traditions and rituals associated with worship.

3. Sacred
Synonyms: Holy, Divine, Revered
Definition: Regarded with great respect and devotion due to

its association with religious or spiritual significance.

Examples:

- The temple is considered a sacred place of worship.

- They preserved the sacred texts for future generations.

- The ceremony included the lighting of candles as a symbol of the sacred.

- The indigenous tribe holds the land as sacred and practices rituals to honor it.

- Sacred music and chants create a meditative atmosphere during ceremonies.

4. Ritual

Synonyms: Ceremony, Rite, Custom

Definition: A formalized set of actions, gestures, or practices performed in a specific order, often with religious or spiritual significance.

Examples:

- The baptism ceremony is an important ritual in many Christian traditions.

- The ritual of breaking bread together symbolizes unity and fellowship.

- The priest conducted the marriage ritual according to the religious customs.

- The morning meditation became an essential part of her daily ritual.

- The ancient civilization had intricate burial rituals to honor the deceased.

5. Prayer

Synonyms: Invocation, Supplication, Petition

Definition: A form of communication with a deity or higher power, often expressing praise, gratitude, or requests.

Examples:

- She begins her day with a moment of prayer and reflection.

- The congregation joined in prayer for healing and peace.

- He offered a heartfelt prayer for the well-being of his family.

- During times of adversity, people often turn to prayer for strength and guidance.
- The prayerful atmosphere in the temple provided a sense of peace and tranquility.

6. Faith

Synonyms: Belief, Trust, Confidence

Definition: Complete trust or confidence in a religious or spiritual system, doctrines, teachings, or higher power.

Examples:
- Her faith in God's plan gives her strength during challenging times.
- The priest delivered a sermon on the importance of faith and perseverance.
- The pilgrimage was an act of faith, seeking spiritual enlightenment.
- He embraced his faith and dedicated himself to serving others.
- The community came together to support each other, united by their shared faith.

7. Salvation

Synonyms: Redemption, Deliverance, Liberation

Definition: The act or process of being saved or protected from harm, sin, or suffering, often associated with religious beliefs.

Examples:
- The concept of salvation is central to many religious traditions.
- They sought spiritual guidance in their search for salvation.
- The preacher spoke about the path to salvation and eternal life.
- The belief in salvation motivates individuals to live a virtuous life.
- The message of hope and salvation resonated with the congregation.

8. Enlightenment

Synonyms: Illumination, Wisdom, Awareness

Definition: The state of attaining deep spiritual or intellectual understanding, often associated with profound insight or awakening.

Examples:

- The meditation retreat aimed to facilitate self-discovery and enlightenment.

- The spiritual leader shared teachings to guide others on the path to enlightenment.

- The seeker embarked on a journey of self-reflection and enlightenment.

- The ancient texts contain wisdom and guidance for those seeking enlightenment.

- The artist expressed his spiritual experiences through paintings that evoke enlightenment.

9. Devotion

Synonyms: Dedication, Loyalty, Commitment

Definition: Strong and deep feelings of love, loyalty, or commitment towards a deity, religious practice, or spiritual path.

Examples:

- Her devotion to her faith is evident in her daily prayers and rituals.

- The monk's life is characterized by a profound devotion to spiritual growth.

- The devotees gathered at the temple to express their devotion and seek blessings.

- The spiritual teacher emphasized the importance of devotion in the journey of self-realization.

- The artist's work is a testament to his devotion to capturing the divine in art.

10. Sacred Texts

Synonyms: Holy Scriptures, Religious Writings, Divine Books

Definition: Written texts or scriptures considered

authoritative and revered within a religious or spiritual tradition.

Examples:

- The Quran is the sacred text of Islam.

- The Bible contains the sacred texts of Christianity.

- The Vedas are the ancient sacred texts of Hinduism.

- Buddhist teachings are found in various sacred texts, including the Tripitaka.

- Scholars study the sacred texts to gain insights into religious beliefs and practices.

11. Meditation

Synonyms: Contemplation, Reflection, Mindfulness

Definition: A practice of focusing the mind and achieving a calm and peaceful state, often used for relaxation, self-reflection, or spiritual growth.

Examples:

- She finds solace and clarity through daily meditation.

- The retreat offered meditation sessions to promote inner peace and self-awareness.

- The monk spends hours in deep meditation as part of his spiritual practice.

- The benefits of meditation include reduced stress and improved mental well-being.

- The guided meditation helped participants cultivate a sense of serenity and mindfulness.

12. Enlightenment

Synonyms: Awakening, Illumination, Realization

Definition: The state of profound spiritual understanding or awareness, often associated with the realization of ultimate truth or self-realization.

Examples:

- The seeker devoted years to the pursuit of enlightenment.

- Many spiritual traditions emphasize the importance of enlightenment as the ultimate goal.

- The teacher shared insights to guide others on the path to enlightenment.
- The experience of enlightenment transformed his perspective on life.
- The ancient texts contain wisdom and teachings on the journey to enlightenment.

13. Ritual

Synonyms: Ceremony, Rite, Tradition

Definition: A formalized set of actions, gestures, or practices performed in a specific order, often associated with religious or spiritual significance.

Examples:
- The wedding ceremony involved traditional rituals and customs.
- The religious ritual is performed annually to commemorate a significant event.
- The ritual of lighting incense symbolizes purification and offering.
- The prayer circle is a ritual practiced by the community for unity and collective intention.
- The rituals and symbols hold deep meaning for the followers of the faith.

14. Faith

Synonyms: Belief, Trust, Conviction

Definition: Strong belief or trust in a higher power, religious doctrine, or spiritual principles.

Examples:
- Her faith provides her with strength and guidance in difficult times.
- The sermon emphasized the importance of faith in times of uncertainty.
- The community gathers in faith to worship and connect with the divine.
- The journey of faith involves seeking meaning and purpose

in life.
- Faith is a personal and deeply held conviction for many individuals.

15. Spirituality

Synonyms: Mysticism, Transcendence, Inner Journey

Definition: The state or quality of being connected to one's inner self, higher power, or the divine, often independent of religious traditions.

Examples:
- She explores spirituality through meditation and self-reflection.
- The retreat offered a space for individuals to deepen their spirituality.
- The spiritual teacher shared practices to cultivate a sense of spirituality.
- Many find solace and inspiration in the exploration of their spirituality.
- Spirituality is a personal journey that can manifest in different ways for each individual.

16. Belief

Synonyms: Faith, Conviction, Trust

Definition: A strong mental acceptance or trust in something, often based on religious or spiritual teachings.

Examples:
- Her belief in the power of positive thinking shapes her daily life.
- The community holds a shared belief in the interconnectedness of all beings.
- The belief in karma motivates individuals to act with compassion and kindness.
- Different cultures have distinct beliefs about the origin of the universe.
- Belief in the existence of a higher power is a central tenet of many religions.

17. Sacredness

Synonyms: Holiness, Sanctity, Divinity

Definition: The quality or state of being regarded as sacred, holy, or divine.

Examples:

- The sacredness of the temple evokes a sense of reverence and awe.
- The ritual is performed with a deep understanding of its sacredness.
- The sacredness of life is honored through rituals and ethical practices.
- The artwork captures the essence and sacredness of the natural world.
- The sacredness of the space creates a peaceful and meditative atmosphere.

18. Morality

Synonyms: Ethics, Virtue, Righteousness

Definition: Principles or standards of right and wrong conduct, often influenced by religious or philosophical beliefs.

Examples:

- Ethical teachings provide a framework for guiding moral decisions.
- The society upholds a strong sense of morality and social responsibility.
- The philosopher explored the concept of morality in his writings.
- The moral values shared across cultures emphasize compassion and justice.
- The discussion focused on the ethical implications of the decision.

19. Compassion

Synonyms: Empathy, Kindness, Benevolence

Definition: Deep awareness of the suffering of others and the desire to alleviate it, often rooted in religious or spiritual teachings.

Examples:

- Practicing compassion towards others is a core value in many faith traditions.

- The act of helping those in need is an expression of compassion.

- The spiritual teacher emphasized the importance of cultivating compassion.

- Compassion and understanding can bridge differences and foster harmony.

- The world would be a better place if more people embraced compassion.

20. Wisdom

Synonyms: Knowledge, Insight, Enlightenment

Definition: Deep understanding and knowledge gained through experience, reflection, and the pursuit of truth.

Examples:

- The wise elder shares his wisdom with the younger generation.

- Ancient texts contain timeless wisdom on living a meaningful life.

- The pursuit of wisdom is a lifelong journey of learning and growth.

- The teacher imparts valuable wisdom through stories and parables.

- She sought the wisdom of the spiritual mentor for guidance in her path.

19. Social Issues

1. Inequality

Synonyms: Disparity, Imbalance, Social disparity

Definition: The state of unfairness or unequal distribution of resources, opportunities, or treatment among individuals or groups in society.

Examples:

- Income inequality is a pressing social issue in many countries.
- The government is working to address educational inequality among marginalized communities.
- Gender inequality continues to persist in various aspects of society.
- The documentary sheds light on the social inequalities faced by marginalized populations.
- Efforts are being made to reduce the wealth gap and promote social equality.

2. Discrimination

Synonyms: Prejudice, Bias, Bigotry

Definition: Unfair or unjust treatment of individuals or groups based on certain characteristics such as race, gender, religion, or ethnicity.

Examples:
- Racial discrimination remains a significant challenge in our society.
- The organization is committed to combating discrimination against LGBTQ+ individuals.
- Discrimination based on physical appearance is a form of social injustice.
- The law prohibits employment discrimination on the basis of age.
- The documentary highlights the experiences of individuals who have faced discrimination.

3. Poverty

Synonyms: Destitution, Impoverishment, Neediness

Definition: The state of extreme lack of financial resources or material possessions, often resulting in poor living conditions and limited opportunities.

Examples:
- Many families struggle to escape the cycle of poverty.
- The government has implemented social programs to

alleviate poverty.
- Poverty rates have increased in the aftermath of the economic recession.
- Lack of access to education perpetuates the cycle of poverty.
- The organization provides support and resources to communities living in poverty.

4. Homelessness
Synonyms: Houselessness, Rooflessness, Displaced
Definition: The condition of lacking a permanent, safe, and adequate place to live, often resulting in individuals or families living on the streets or in temporary shelters.
Examples:
- The city is grappling with the issue of homelessness and affordable housing.
- The organization works to provide shelter and support to the homeless population.
- Homelessness is a complex issue with multiple underlying causes.
- Many homeless individuals face challenges in accessing healthcare and social services.
- Efforts are being made to address the root causes of homelessness.

5. Social justice
Synonyms: Equity, Fairness, Equality
Definition: The concept of fair and just treatment of individuals and groups in society, ensuring equal rights, opportunities, and access to resources.
Examples:
- The movement advocates for social justice and equal rights for all.
- The organization works towards achieving social justice through policy reform.
- Social justice requires addressing systemic inequalities and biases.

- The court ruling was seen as a victory for social justice and human rights.
- The government's commitment to social justice is reflected in its policies and programs.

6. Marginalization

Synonyms: Exclusion, Alienation, Disadvantaged

Definition: The process of pushing certain individuals or groups to the edges or margins of society, limiting their access to resources, opportunities, and decision-making power.

Examples:
- The marginalized communities are often denied basic rights and services.
- Marginalization of minority groups is a concern in many societies.
- The organization aims to empower marginalized youth through education and support.
- Policies that perpetuate marginalization need to be challenged and reformed.
- The documentary sheds light on the experiences of marginalized individuals.

7. Social activism

Synonyms: Advocacy, Protest, Social advocacy

Definition: The efforts and actions taken by individuals or groups to bring about social and political change, raise awareness, and advocate for specific causes or issues.

Examples:
- Social activism plays a crucial role in addressing societal injustices.
- The youth-led movement is at the forefront of social activism for climate action.
- The organization engages in social activism to promote human rights.
- Social media has become a powerful tool for mobilizing social activism.

- The protests are a manifestation of widespread social activism.

8. Diversity

Synonyms: Variety, Multiculturalism, Plurality

Definition: The presence of different cultures, ethnicities, religions, and identities within a society, promoting inclusivity and tolerance.

Examples:

- Embracing diversity enriches our society and fosters understanding.
- The workplace values diversity and promotes equal opportunities.
- Cultural diversity contributes to the vibrant fabric of our society.
- The school curriculum includes lessons on diversity and inclusion.
- The event celebrates the diversity of artistic expressions.

9. Inclusion

Synonyms: Incorporation, Integration, Embracing

Definition: The action or policy of ensuring that individuals of diverse backgrounds, identities, or abilities are valued, respected, and fully involved in all aspects of society.

Examples:

- Inclusion is an essential aspect of creating a harmonious and equal society.
- The organization promotes inclusivity through diverse representation.
- The school fosters a culture of inclusion and acceptance.
- Accessible facilities and accommodations enhance inclusion for people with disabilities.
- Inclusion requires challenging discriminatory attitudes and practices.

10. Social inequality

Synonyms: Disparity, Social imbalance, Unequal distribution

Definition: The unequal distribution of resources, opportunities, and privileges in society, leading to disparities and disadvantages for certain individuals or groups.

Examples:

- Social inequality hinders equal access to education and healthcare.

- The widening wealth gap is a significant driver of social inequality.

- Systemic factors contribute to persistent social inequality.

- Policies that address social inequality are essential for a just society.

- The documentary explores the consequences of social inequality.

11. Social responsibility

Synonyms: Civic duty, Ethical responsibility, Community engagement

Definition: The moral obligation of individuals and organizations to act in ways that benefit society and contribute to the well-being of others.

Examples:

- Businesses have a social responsibility to prioritize environmental sustainability.

- Volunteering is an expression of social responsibility and community engagement.

- The government is accountable for upholding social responsibility in policymaking.

- Education plays a vital role in fostering a sense of social responsibility in individuals.

- Social responsibility requires individuals to consider the impact of their actions on others.

12. Human rights

Synonyms: Civil liberties, Fundamental rights, Basic freedoms

Definition: Inherent rights and freedoms to which all

individuals are entitled, regardless of their background, race, gender, or beliefs.

Examples:

- The organization advocates for the protection of human rights worldwide.

- Human rights violations continue to be a global concern.

- The Universal Declaration of Human Rights affirms the principles of equality and justice.

- Education is key to raising awareness about human rights and promoting social change.

- The court ruling upheld the individual's right to freedom of speech, a fundamental human right.

13. Civil rights

Synonyms: Equal rights, Legal rights, Citizenship rights

Definition: The rights and privileges granted to individuals as members of a society, ensuring equal treatment, protection, and opportunities under the law.

Examples:

- The civil rights movement fought for racial equality and social justice.

- The constitution guarantees the protection of civil rights for all citizens

.

- Voting rights are a fundamental aspect of civil rights in a democratic society.

- The organization advocates for the expansion of civil rights for marginalized communities.

- The court decision marked a significant victory for civil rights in the country.

14. Social cohesion

Synonyms: Unity, Harmony, Solidarity

Definition: The sense of togetherness, cooperation, and mutual support among individuals and communities within a society, leading to social stability and resilience.

Examples:
- Social cohesion is essential for a peaceful and inclusive society.
- The community works together to promote social cohesion and address common challenges.
- Social programs and initiatives foster social cohesion by bridging divides.
- Interfaith dialogue promotes understanding and social cohesion among different religious groups.
- The festival celebrates the diversity and social cohesion of the local community.

15. Empowerment
Synonyms: Enablement, Strengthening, Self-empowerment
Definition: The process of providing individuals or communities with the tools, resources, and opportunities to enhance their abilities, confidence, and decision-making power.
Examples:
- Education is a powerful tool for the empowerment of individuals.
- The organization empowers marginalized youth through mentorship and skill development.
- Economic empowerment is crucial for breaking the cycle of poverty.
- Empowerment programs aim to give voice to marginalized communities.
- The workshop focused on building self-esteem and empowerment in young girls.

16. Social welfare
Synonyms: Social support, Public assistance, Welfare services
Definition: The collective efforts, policies, and programs aimed at promoting the well-being and quality of life of individuals and communities, particularly those in need or vulnerable situations.
Examples:

- The government invests in social welfare programs to provide support to disadvantaged populations.
- Access to healthcare is a fundamental aspect of social welfare.
- The organization works to improve social welfare through community development projects.
- Social welfare policies aim to address social inequalities and promote social justice.
- The conference discussed strategies for enhancing social welfare in urban areas.

17. Community engagement

Synonyms: Community involvement, Civic participation, Active citizenship

Definition: The active participation, collaboration, and contribution of individuals within a community to address common issues, promote social change, and enhance the overall well-being of the community.

Examples:
- Community engagement is key to fostering a sense of belonging and social cohesion.
- The organization encourages community engagement through volunteer programs.
- The project's success relies on the active community engagement and input.
- Community engagement initiatives aim to empower residents and address local challenges.
- The town hall meeting served as a platform for community engagement and dialogue.

18. Social norms

Synonyms: Cultural norms, Societal conventions, Accepted behavior

Definition: The shared expectations, beliefs, values, and behaviors that shape the accepted and appropriate conduct within a society or social group.

Examples:
- Social norms vary across different cultures and societies.
- Challenging social norms can lead to societal progress and positive change.
- The media plays a significant role in shaping and reinforcing social norms.
- The campaign aims to shift social norms around gender stereotypes.
- Understanding social norms is important for effective cross-cultural communication.

19. Stigma
Synonyms: Discrimination, Social disgrace, Stereotyping
Definition: The negative attitudes, beliefs, and prejudices held by society towards individuals or groups based on certain characteristics or circumstances, leading to social exclusion and marginalization.
Examples:
- Mental health stigma remains a barrier to seeking help and support.
- The organization works to reduce the stigma associated with addiction and recovery.
- Stigma surrounding HIV/AIDS can have detrimental effects on affected individuals.
- The campaign aims to challenge the stigma around disabilities and promote inclusivity.
- Overcoming stigma requires education, awareness, and empathy.

20. Social change
Synonyms: Societal transformation, Progressive change, Cultural shift
Definition: The process of significant and lasting transformation in social structures, attitudes, behaviors, and norms within a society, leading to improved conditions and addressing social issues.

Examples:

- Grassroots movements have the power to drive social change.

- Social media has become a catalyst for mobilizing and amplifying social change.

- The organization's mission is to create positive social change through advocacy and awareness.

- The civil rights movement brought about significant social change in the country.

- Art can be a powerful tool for inspiring social change and challenging perceptions.

20. Prefixes and Suffixes

1. Un-
   Synonyms: Not, Non-, In-
   Definition: A prefix used to indicate negation, lack, or reversal.
   Examples:
   - She was unhappy with the decision.
   - The company implemented an unconventional marketing strategy.
   - The professor emphasized the importance of unbiased research.

2. Dis-
   Synonyms: Un-, Anti-, De-
   Definition: A prefix used to indicate negation, reversal, or removal.
   Examples:
   - The manager disagreed with the proposed plan.
   - The committee decided to discontinue the project.
   - The detective discovered new evidence that disproved the suspect's alibi.

3. Re-
   Synonyms: Again, Back, Return
   Definition: A prefix used to indicate repetition, restoration, or reversal.
   Examples:
   - She revised her essay before submitting it.
   - The team reassembled after a brief break.
   - The company relocated its headquarters to the original city.

4. Pre-
   Synonyms: Before, Prior, Preceding
   Definition: A prefix used to indicate before or in advance.
   Examples:
   - The students prepared for the upcoming exam.
   - The company held a pre-meeting to discuss the agenda.

- The prehistoric era predates the existence of humans.

5. Post-
   Synonyms: After, Following, Subsequent
   Definition: A prefix used to indicate after or later.
   Examples:
   - She posted a message on social media after the event.
   - The participants completed a post-workshop survey.
   - The postgraduate program focuses on advanced research.

6. Mis-
   Synonyms: Wrong, Incorrect, Faulty
   Definition: A prefix used to indicate error, wrongness, or misunderstanding.
   Examples:
   - The student misunderstood the assignment instructions.
   - The reporter misquoted the interviewee's statement.
   - The actor's performance received mixed reviews.

7. In-
   Synonyms: Not, Un-, Non-
   Definition: A prefix used to indicate negation, lack, or opposite.
   Examples:
   - The company invested in innovative technology.
   - The medication is ineffective for treating the condition.
   - The professor emphasized the importance of inclusivity.

8. Pro-
   Synonyms: Forward, For, In favor of
   Definition: A prefix used to indicate support, promotion, or advocacy.
   Examples:
   - The organization promotes environmental sustainability.
   - The speaker presented a pro-argument for the proposed policy.
   - The proponent of the idea highlighted its potential benefits.

9. Ex-

Synonyms: Former, Previous, Out of

Definition: A prefix used to indicate former or previous status.

Examples:

- The ex-president delivered a speech at the conference.
- The employee exhibited exceptional leadership skills.
- The ex-student returned to the university for a reunion.

10. Co-

Synonyms: With, Together, Jointly

Definition: A prefix used to indicate joint or cooperative action.

Examples:

- The colleagues collaborated on a research project.
- The conference brought together co-authors from different countries.
- The company organized a co-sponsored event with a partner organization.

11. Semi-

Synonyms: Half, Partial, Incomplete

Definition: A prefix used to indicate partial or incomplete status.

Examples:

- She attended a semi-annual meeting of the organization.
- The company introduced a semi-automatic version of the product.
- The singer performed a semi-acoustic version of the song.

12. Sub-

Synonyms: Under

, Below, Lesser

Definition: A prefix used to indicate below, under, or subordinate to.

Examples:

- The submarine explored the depths of the ocean.

- The students submitted their assignments before the deadline.
- The company launched a sub-brand targeting a specific market segment.

13. Inter-

Synonyms: Between, Among, Mutual

Definition: A prefix used to indicate between, among, or mutual interaction.

Examples:

- The international conference brought together experts from various fields.
- The interdisciplinary research project involved collaboration between scientists and engineers.
- The internet facilitates interconnectivity and communication across the globe.

14. Hyper-

Synonyms: Over, Excessive, Extreme

Definition: A prefix used to indicate excessive, beyond, or above normal.

Examples:

- The hyperactive child had difficulty sitting still in class.
- The company experienced a hypergrowth phase, expanding rapidly.
- The athlete achieved a new personal record, displaying hyperperformance.

15. En-

Synonyms: Cause to, Make, Provide with

Definition: A prefix used to indicate to cause, make, or provide with.

Examples:

- The company employed environmentally-friendly practices to ensure sustainability.
- The speaker encouraged the audience to engage in the conversation.

- The project manager enabled the team with the necessary resources.

16. Anti-

Synonyms: Against, Opposed to, Contrary to
Definition: A prefix used to indicate opposition or contrary to.
Examples:
- The activists organized an anti-war protest.
- The company developed an anti-virus software to protect against cyber threats.
- The students participated in an anti-bullying campaign.

17. Un-

Synonyms: Not, Non-, In-
Definition: A prefix used to indicate negation, lack, or reversal.
Examples:
- She was unhappy with the decision.
- The company implemented an unconventional marketing strategy.
- The professor emphasized the importance of unbiased research.

18. Im-

Synonyms: Not, Un-, Non-
Definition: A prefix used to indicate negation, lack, or opposite.
Examples:
- The employee was impressed by her impeccable work ethic.
- The project faced numerous impediments that delayed its completion.
- The medication is contraindicated for patients with certain medical conditions.

19. Over-

Synonyms: Excessive, Too much, Surpassing
Definition: A prefix used to indicate excess, beyond, or

surpassing.

Examples:

- The overconfident speaker failed to acknowledge other perspectives.

- The company experienced an overload of customer inquiries.

- The project went overbudget due to unforeseen expenses.

20. Multi-

Synonyms: Many, Multiple, Several

Definition: A prefix used to indicate many, multiple, or several.

Examples:

- The company operates in multiple countries around the world.

- The multifaceted problem requires a comprehensive approach.

- The musician demonstrated multitasking skills by playing multiple instruments simultaneously.

21. Film and Cinema

1. Blockbuster
   Synonyms: Hit, Smash, Success
   Definition: A highly successful and widely popular film.
   Examples:
   - The new superhero movie became a blockbuster at the box office.
   - The film's impressive special effects contributed to its blockbuster status.
   - The studio invested a significant budget to create a potential blockbuster.

2. Genre
   Synonyms: Category, Type, Style
   Definition: A specific category or style of film characterized by common themes or storytelling conventions.
   Examples:
   - She enjoys watching films in the horror genre.
   - The director is known for his work in the comedy genre.
   - The film festival showcased a diverse range of genres, including drama, romance, and documentary.

3. Plot
   Synonyms: Storyline, Narrative, Scenario
   Definition: The sequence of events that unfold in a film, including the main storyline and subplots.
   Examples:
   - The film's plot revolves around a detective solving a mysterious crime.
   - The plot twist in the movie caught the audience by surprise.
   - The complex plot of the film kept the viewers engaged until the end.

4. Sequel
   Synonyms: Follow-up, Continuation, Next installment
   Definition: A film that continues the story of a previously

released film, often featuring the same characters or settings.
Examples:
- The highly anticipated sequel to the blockbuster was released this summer.
- The studio announced plans for a sequel to the critically acclaimed film.
- The sequel received mixed reviews from both critics and audiences.

5. Remake
Synonyms: Adaptation, Reimagining, Reboot
Definition: A film that is based on an earlier film, often with a different cast or updated storytelling approach.
Examples:
- The director decided to remake the classic film with a modern twist.
- The remake of the foreign film introduced the story to a new audience.
- The studio announced the casting choices for the upcoming remake.

6. Cast
Synonyms: Actors, Performers, Players
Definition: The group of actors who portray the characters in a film.
Examples:
- The film features a talented cast of award-winning actors.
- The casting director conducted auditions to find the perfect cast for the film.
- The chemistry among the cast members contributed to the film's success.

7. Director
Synonyms: Filmmaker, Filmdirector, Movie director
Definition: The person responsible for overseeing the creative aspects of a film, including guiding the actors and making artistic decisions.

Examples:
- The director won an Academy Award for his exceptional work on the film.
- The director's vision and style are evident in every scene of the movie.
- The director collaborated closely with the cinematographer to achieve the desired visual aesthetic.

8. Cinematography
Synonyms: Filmography, Photography, Visuals
Definition: The art and technique of capturing images on film or digitally, including the use of lighting, camera angles, and composition.
Examples:
- The film's breathtaking cinematography created a visually stunning experience.
- The cinematographer used innovative techniques to capture the essence of the story.
- The film received praise for its remarkable cinematography and visual storytelling.

9. Screenplay
Synonyms: Script, Dialogue, Written work
Definition: The written text of a film, including the dialogue, scene descriptions, and stage directions.
Examples:
- The screenwriter spent months crafting the screenplay for the film.
- The film's screenplay was praised for its compelling dialogue and character development.
- The actors improvised some lines during filming, adding spontaneity to the screenplay.

10. Premiere
Synonyms: Debut, Opening, First showing
Definition: The first public screening of a film, often attended by the cast, crew, and invited guests.

Examples:

- The film had its world premiere at the prestigious film festival.

- The director gave a speech at the film's premiere, expressing gratitude to everyone involved.

- Fans eagerly awaited the premiere of the highly anticipated sequel.

11. Box office

Synonyms: Ticket sales, Revenue, Box office earnings

Definition: The financial success or performance of a film measured by the amount of money earned from ticket sales.

Examples:

- The film broke box office records, becoming the highest-grossing movie of the year.

- Despite receiving positive reviews, the film underperformed at the box office.

- The studio closely monitored the film's box office numbers to determine its success.

12. Critic

Synonyms: Reviewer, Analyst, Evaluator

Definition: A person who professionally analyzes and assesses films, offering opinions and critiques.

Examples:

- The film received rave reviews from critics, praising the performances and storytelling.

- The critic's review of the movie influenced the audience's perception and interest.

- The film's director responded to the critic's comments during an interview.

13. Plot twist

Synonyms: Surprise, Unexpected turn, Twist of events

Definition: A sudden and unexpected change or revelation in the plot of a film, often altering the audience's understanding of the story.

Examples:
- The film's plot twist shocked the audience and kept them guessing until the end.
- The cleverly executed plot twist added depth and complexity to the storyline.
- The film's marketing campaign emphasized the presence of a mind-bending plot twist.

14. Special effects

Synonyms: Visual effects, VFX, CGI

Definition: Technological and artistic techniques used in films to create illusions or enhance visual elements.

Examples:
- The film employed groundbreaking special effects to bring the fantastical world to life.
- The team of visual effects artists meticulously crafted the film's stunning CGI sequences.
- The film won an Academy Award for its exceptional use of special effects.

15. Soundtrack

Synonyms: Score, Music, Sound composition

Definition: The music and audio elements accompanying a film, including the original score, songs, and sound effects.

Examples:
- The film's soundtrack perfectly complemented the emotional tone of each scene.
- The composer created a memorable soundtrack that became iconic in the film industry.
- The soundtrack album of the movie topped the music charts for several weeks.

16. Costume

Synonyms: Outfit, Attire, Dress

Definition: The clothing and accessories worn by actors to portray characters in a film.

Examples:

- The film's costume designer meticulously researched the historical period for accurate costumes.
- The elaborate costumes in the movie showcased the opulence of the era.
- The actress received an award nomination for her outstanding performance and authentic costumes.

17. Set

Synonyms: Stage, Scene, Location

Definition: The physical environment or surroundings where the film is shot, including the constructed or decorated locations.

Examples:
- The film's production designer created intricate sets to transport the audience to different worlds.
- The director chose real-life locations to provide authenticity to the film's setting.
- The set decorators meticulously arranged the props and furnishings to create a realistic ambiance.

18. Editing

Synonyms: Cutting, Trimming, Post-production

Definition: The process of selecting, arranging, and manipulating footage to create the final version of a film.

Examples:
- The film editor skillfully crafted the pacing and rhythm of the movie through precise editing.
- The director collaborated closely with the editor to ensure the film's narrative flowed seamlessly.
- The editing techniques used in the film added suspense and heightened the emotional impact.

19. Dialogue

Synonyms: Conversation, Discourse, Verbal exchange

Definition: The spoken words between characters in a film, encompassing conversations, discussions, and monologues.

Examples:

- The film's dialogue was witty and filled with memorable quotes.
- The screenwriter's ability to write natural and engaging dialogue contributed to the film's success.
- The actors rehearsed the dialogue to ensure delivery and timing were on point.

20. Cinematic

Synonyms: Filmic, Movie-like, Cinematographic

Definition: Pertaining to the art, techniques, or qualities associated with filmmaking or the cinema.

Examples:
- The film showcased breathtaking cinematic visuals that transported the audience to another world.
- The director's unique cinematic style was evident in every frame of the movie.
- The film critic praised the director's ability to create a truly cinematic experience.

22. Geography

1. Terrain

Synonyms: Landscape, Topography, Ground

Definition: The physical features and characteristics of an area of land.

Examples:

- The rugged terrain of the mountainous region made hiking challenging.

- The desert terrain was harsh and inhospitable to most forms of life.

- The expedition team studied the terrain carefully before planning their route.

2. Peninsula

Synonyms: Cape, Promontory, Spit

Definition: A piece of land that is almost completely surrounded by water but connected to the mainland.

Examples:

- The Iberian Peninsula includes Spain and Portugal.

- The Baja California Peninsula extends southwards from the U.S. state of California.

- The Korean Peninsula is located in East Asia, with North Korea and South Korea.

3. Archipelago

Synonyms: Island group, Island chain, Island cluster

Definition: A group or chain of islands.

Examples:

- The Philippine archipelago consists of over 7,000 islands.

- The Greek archipelago is renowned for its beautiful beaches and ancient ruins.

- The Maldives archipelago is a popular destination for honeymooners.

4. Delta

Synonyms: Estuary, Mouth, River mouth

Definition: A triangular-shaped deposit of sediment formed at the mouth of a river.

Examples:

- The Nile Delta in Egypt is an agriculturally fertile region.

- The Mississippi River delta in Louisiana is prone to flooding.

- The Ganges-Brahmaputra Delta is one of the largest river deltas in the world.

5. Plateau

Synonyms: Mesa, Tableland, Upland

Definition: A flat or gently sloping elevated landform with steep sides.

Examples:

- The Colorado Plateau in the United States is known for its stunning canyons and rock formations.

- The Deccan Plateau in India has a predominantly dry and arid climate.

- The Tibetan Plateau is often referred to as the "Roof of the World."

6. Fjord

Synonyms: Inlet, Sound, Bay

Definition: A long, narrow, deep inlet of the sea between high cliffs, typically formed by glacial activity.

Examples:

- The Norwegian fjords attract tourists from around the world with their breathtaking beauty.

- The Milford Sound in New Zealand is a famous fjord renowned for its scenic landscapes.

- The Sognefjord is the longest fjord in Norway.

7. Oasis

Synonyms: Refuge, Haven, Sanctuary

Definition: A fertile area in a desert where water is found, often surrounded by vegetation.

Examples:

- The Sahara Desert is dotted with small oases that provide

sustenance for nomadic tribes.
- The palm tree oasis provided a welcome respite for weary travelers in the arid landscape.
- The desert oasis was a lush green paradise amidst the harsh surroundings.

8. Tundra
Synonyms: Arctic, Frozen, Barren
Definition: A vast, treeless Arctic or alpine biome characterized by permanently frozen subsoil.
Examples:
- The Arctic tundra is home to unique wildlife such as polar bears and reindeer.
- The tundra landscape is marked by low-lying vegetation and frozen lakes.
- The harsh conditions of the tundra make it challenging for plants and animals to survive.

9. Strait
Synonyms: Channel, Passage, Waterway
Definition: A narrow passage of water connecting two larger bodies of water.
Examples:
- The Strait of Gibraltar separates Europe from Africa.
- The Strait of Hormuz is a critical waterway for global oil transportation.
- The Bering Strait separates Russia and Alaska.

10. Savanna
Synonyms: Grassland, Prairie, Steppe
Definition: A tropical or subtropical grassland ecosystem characterized by scattered trees and grasses.
Examples:
- The African savanna is known for its diverse wildlife, including lions, elephants, and giraffes.
- The Australian savanna is home to unique species like kangaroos and emus.

- The Serengeti National Park in Tanzania is a famous savanna habitat.

11. Peninsula
Synonyms: Cape, Promontory, Spit
Definition: A piece of land that is almost completely surrounded by water but connected to the mainland.
Examples:
- The Italian Peninsula is home to the country of Italy.
- The Yucatan Peninsula in Mexico is a popular tourist destination.
- The Iberian Peninsula includes Spain and Portugal.

12. Glacial
Synonyms: Frozen, Polar, Icy
Definition: Relating to or produced by glaciers.
Examples:
- The glacial ice carved out deep valleys and fjords in the landscape.
- The retreat of the glacial mass revealed the formation of moraines.
- The glacial meltwater feeds into the rivers and lakes in the region.

13. Estuary
Synonyms: Inlet, Delta, Bay
Definition: The tidal mouth of a large river where it meets the sea, characterized by mixing of freshwater and saltwater.
Examples:
- The Chesapeake Bay in the United States is an estuary where the Susquehanna River meets the Atlantic Ocean.
- The Ganges Delta in Bangladesh is an estuarine region rich in biodiversity.
- The Thames Estuary in England is a major shipping and trading hub.

14. Crater

Synonyms: Hollow, Cavity, Pit
Definition: A bowl-shaped depression or cavity, often found at the summit or on the sides of a volcano.
Examples:
- The volcanic crater was filled with hot bubbling lava.
- The impact crater was evidence of a meteorite strike.
- The hiking trail led to the rim of the crater, offering panoramic views of the surrounding landscape.

15. Wetland
Synonyms: Marsh, Swamp, Bog
Definition: An area of land where water covers the soil or is present near the surface, supporting unique plant and animal life.
Examples:
- The Everglades in Florida is a famous wetland ecosystem.
- The wetland habitat provides nesting grounds for migratory birds.
- The conservation efforts aim to protect and restore wetlands for their ecological importance.

16. Dune
Synonyms: Sandhill, Drift, Mound
Definition: A hill or ridge of sand formed by wind or water action.
Examples:
- The sand dunes stretched for miles along the coastline.
- The camel trudged across the vast desert dunes.
- The shifting dunes created a constantly changing landscape.

17. Lagoon
Synonyms: Lake, Pond, Pool
Definition: A shallow body of water separated from a larger body of water by a barrier such as a sandbar or coral reef.
Examples:
- The turquoise lagoon was a popular spot for snorkeling and swimming.

- The resort overlooked a peaceful lagoon surrounded by palm trees.
- The lagoon teemed with colorful fish and coral formations.

18. Rift

Synonyms: Fissure, Crack, Gap

Definition: A long, narrow crack or opening that forms due to tectonic movement.

Examples:

- The Great Rift Valley in Africa is a geologically significant rift.
- The rift in the glacier indicated the movement of ice.
- The earthquake created a rift in the ground, causing structural damage.

19. Coral reef

Synonyms: Atoll, Cnidarian, Coral colony

Definition: A marine ecosystem formed by the accumulation and growth of coral polyps.

Examples:

- The Great Barrier Reef in Australia is the largest coral reef system in the world.
- Snorkelers and divers explored the vibrant coral reef, spotting colorful fish and marine life.
- The conservation efforts aimed to protect the delicate balance of the coral reef ecosystem.

20. Geothermal

Synonyms: Thermal, Heat, Volcanic

Definition: Relating to the heat generated and stored within the Earth's interior.

Examples:

- The geothermal energy was harnessed for heating and electricity production.
- The hot springs were a result of geothermal activity.
- The geothermal region provided a unique opportunity to study Earth's thermal processes.

21. Erosion

Synonyms: Weathering, Corrosion, Abrasion

Definition: The gradual wearing away or removal of soil, rock, or land surface by natural forces such as wind, water, or ice.

Examples:

- The river's strong currents caused erosion along its banks.

- The coastal erosion threatened the stability of the cliffs.

- The effects of erosion were visible in the exposed rock formations.

22. Geology

Synonyms: Earth science, Earth history, Geological science

Definition: The study of the Earth's solid materials, including rocks, minerals, and the processes that shape the Earth's structure.

Examples:

- The geology field trip involved examining rock formations and studying their composition.

- The geology professor explained the geological history of the region.

- The geological survey aimed to map the different layers of rock in the area.

23. Rift

Synonyms: Fissure, Split, Crack

Definition: A large crack or opening in the Earth's crust, often associated with tectonic plate movements.

Examples:

- The rift was evidence of the underlying geologic activity.

- The continental rift formed as a result of diverging tectonic plates.

- The geologists monitored the rift for any signs of increased seismic activity.

24. Cartography

Synonyms: Mapmaking, Map drawing, Charting

Definition: The art and science of creating maps and charts.

Examples:

- The cartographer created detailed maps of the mountainous region.

- The advancements in cartography led to more accurate navigation.

- The cartography department worked on updating the city's street maps.

25. Crust

Synonyms: Earth's surface, Earth's outer layer, Earth's shell

Definition: The outermost layer of the Earth's solid surface, consisting of rocks and minerals.

Examples:

- The Earth's crust is divided into several tectonic plates.

- The crust is thickest beneath the continents and thinner beneath the oceans.

- The geologists studied the composition and structure of the crust.

23. LAW AND JUSTICE

1. Legislation
   Synonyms: Laws, Statutes, Regulations
   Definition: The act or process of making or enacting laws.
   Examples:
   - The government passed new legislation to protect consumers' rights.
   - The legislation aims to address issues of discrimination in the workplace.
   - The proposed legislation will have a significant impact on the healthcare system.

2. Judiciary
   Synonyms: Judicial system, Courts, Legal system
   Definition: The branch of government that interprets and applies the law.
   Examples:
   - The independence of the judiciary is crucial for upholding the rule of law.
   - The judiciary plays a vital role in ensuring justice is served.
   - The judge's decision was based on the principles of the judiciary.

3. Jurisdiction
   Synonyms: Authority, Power, Control
   Definition: The official power to make legal decisions and judgments within a specific area or territory.
   Examples:
   - The court has jurisdiction over cases involving federal law.
   - The police officer acted within their jurisdiction when making the arrest.
   - The jurisdiction of the local government extends to zoning regulations.

4. Defendant

Synonyms: Accused, Respondent, Offender

Definition: A person who is accused of a crime and brought to trial.

Examples:

- The defendant pleaded not guilty to the charges.

- The defense attorney questioned the credibility of the prosecution's evidence.

- The defendant's rights must be protected throughout the legal process.

5. Plaintiff

Synonyms: Complainant, Claimant, Accuser

Definition: A person who brings a legal action against another in a court of law.

Examples:

- The plaintiff filed a lawsuit against the company for breach of contract.

- The plaintiff's attorney presented compelling evidence to support their case.

- The plaintiff seeks compensation for damages caused by the defendant.

6. Evidence

Synonyms: Proof, Testimony, Documentation

Definition: Information or material that is used to support or prove a claim or argument.

Examples:

- The prosecution presented compelling evidence linking the defendant to the crime.

- The defense attorney challenged the credibility of the presented evidence.

- The judge ruled that the evidence was inadmissible due to improper handling.

7. Verdict

Synonyms: Judgment, Decision, Ruling

Definition: The final decision or outcome reached by a jury or judge in a legal case.

Examples:

- The jury deliberated for hours before reaching a unanimous verdict.
- The judge delivered a guilty verdict based on the evidence presented.
- The verdict was met with mixed reactions from the public.

8. Trial

Synonyms: Court case, Legal proceeding, Hearing

Definition: A formal examination of evidence before a judge and, in some cases, a jury, to determine the guilt or innocence of a person accused of a crime.

Examples:

- The high-profile trial attracted widespread media attention.
- The defense attorney cross-examined the witnesses during the trial.
- The trial lasted for several weeks, with both sides presenting their arguments.

9. Advocate

Synonyms: Champion, Supporter, Defender

Definition: A person who publicly supports or argues for a particular cause or policy.

Examples:

- The lawyer served as an advocate for the defendant, ensuring their rights were protected.
- The organization advocates for the rights of marginalized communities.
- The advocate spoke passionately about the need for criminal justice reform.

10. Sentencing

Synonyms: Punishment, Penalty, Judgment

Definition: The act or process of imposing a punishment on a person convicted of a crime.

Examples:

- The judge considered various factors when determining the appropriate sentencing.

- The sentencing guidelines provide a framework for judges to determine penalties.

- The severity of the crime influenced the length of the sentencing.

11. Constitutional

Synonyms: Legal, Statutory, Institutional

Definition: Relating to the principles and rules outlined in a constitution.

Examples:

- The court analyzed whether the law was in line with constitutional rights.

- The constitutional amendment protected freedom of speech.

- The constitutionality of the new policy was questioned by civil rights groups.

12. Habeas corpus

Synonyms: Writ of liberty, Legal protection, Right to challenge detention

Definition: A legal action or writ that requires a person under arrest to be brought before a judge or into court, especially to secure their release unless lawful grounds are shown for their detention.

Examples:

- The lawyer filed a writ of habeas corpus on behalf of the detainee.

- The judge granted the habeas corpus petition, ordering the immediate release of the prisoner.

- The habeas corpus safeguarded the individual's right to challenge their imprisonment.

13. Due process

Synonyms: Fairness, Justice, Procedural rights

Definition: The principle that ensures a fair and impartial legal process, where individuals have the right to be heard and have their rights protected.

Examples:

- The accused has the right to due process, including legal representation and a fair trial.

- The court emphasized the importance of upholding due process in all cases.

- The due process guarantees the accused the opportunity to present their defense.

14. Injunction

Synonyms: Restraining order, Prohibition, Ban

Definition: A court order that prohibits or requires a specific action or behavior.

Examples:

- The court issued an injunction preventing the company from continuing its illegal activities.

- The environmental group sought an injunction to halt the construction of the pipeline.

- The injunction was lifted after the company demonstrated compliance with environmental regulations.

15. Parole

Synonyms: Release, Conditional release, Probation

Definition: The conditional release of a prisoner before the completion of their sentence, under specific terms and supervision.

Examples:

- The parole board granted early release to the inmate based on their good behavior.

- The parolee must regularly report to their assigned parole officer.

- The conditions of parole include regular drug testing and mandatory counseling.

16. Litigation

Synonyms: Lawsuit, Legal action, Legal dispute

Definition: The process of taking legal action through the courts to resolve a dispute.

Examples:

- The parties involved in the dispute opted for litigation rather than mediation.
- The litigation process can be lengthy and expensive.
- The attorney prepared the necessary documents for the initiation of litigation.

17. Defendant

Synonyms: Accused, Respondent, Offender

Definition: A person who is accused of a crime and brought to trial.

Examples:

- The defendant pleaded not guilty to the charges.
- The defense attorney questioned the credibility of the prosecution's evidence.
- The defendant's rights must be protected throughout the legal process.

18. Compensation

Synonyms: Restitution, Reimbursement, Damages

Definition: Payment or other benefits provided to someone as a result of suffering injury, loss, or inconvenience.

Examples:

- The victim sought compensation for the physical and emotional damages caused by the accident.
- The court awarded substantial compensation to the plaintiff for the wrongful termination.
- The compensation package included salary, benefits, and stock options.

19. Juror

Synonyms: Jury member, Panelist, Assessor

Definition: A member of a jury who listens to the evidence presented in a trial and helps reach a verdict.

Examples:

- The juror carefully considered the facts of the case before reaching a decision.

- The judge instructed the jurors to base their verdict solely on the evidence presented.

- The juror was excused due to a conflict of interest.

20. Appeal

Synonyms: Challenge, Review, Protest

Definition: The process of requesting a higher court to review and reconsider a decision made by a lower court.

Examples:

- The defendant filed an appeal to overturn the conviction and seek a new trial.

- The appellate court agreed to hear the appeal based on new evidence.

- The appeal was dismissed due to a lack of substantial grounds.

24. MEDIA AND COMMUNICATION

1. Broadcast

Synonyms: Air, Transmit, Telecast

Definition: To transmit or distribute audio or video content through radio, television, or online platforms.

Examples:

- The news was broadcast live on national television.

- The radio station broadcasts news updates every hour.

- The event will be broadcasted globally via streaming platforms.

2. Journalism

Synonyms: News reporting, Reporting, News media

Definition: The activity of collecting, verifying, and presenting news and information through various media channels.

Examples:

- She pursued a career in journalism and became a news reporter.

- The journalist conducted interviews to gather information for the article.

- The importance of unbiased journalism in a democratic society cannot be understated.

3. Editorial

Synonyms: Opinion piece, Commentary, Column

Definition: An article or commentary expressing the opinion or viewpoint of the author or publication.

Examples:

- The editorial criticized the government's handling of the situation.

- The newspaper's editorial called for stricter environmental regulations.

- The editorial section of the magazine features diverse perspectives on current issues.

4. Censorship

Synonyms: Suppression, Control, Restraint

Definition: The act of restricting or prohibiting the dissemination of information, ideas, or artistic expression.

Examples:

- The government imposed censorship on the controversial film.
- Internet censorship is a topic of debate in many countries.
- The artist's work faced censorship due to its explicit content.

5. Press release

Synonyms: Media release, News release, Statement

Definition: A written or recorded communication directed at news media, announcing newsworthy information or updates.

Examples:

- The company issued a press release to announce its new product launch.
- The press release provided details about the upcoming event.
- The politician's press release addressed recent policy changes.

6. Publicity

Synonyms: Promotion, Exposure, Public attention

Definition: The act of creating awareness and attracting attention from the public through media coverage.

Examples:

- The celebrity's new film received significant publicity in the media.
- The company hired a public relations team to generate positive publicity.
- The event organizers sought publicity through social media campaigns.

7. Advertising

Synonyms: Marketing, Promotion, Commercialization

Definition: The activity of promoting a product, service, or idea through paid communication channels.

Examples:

- The company invested heavily in advertising to reach a wider audience.

- The television commercial showcased the benefits of the new product.

- Online advertising has become a dominant form of marketing.

8. Headline

Synonyms: Title, Heading, Caption

Definition: A brief and attention-grabbing summary of a news article or story.

Examples:

- The newspaper headline captured the essence of the breaking news.

- The headline of the magazine article intrigued readers to dive deeper.

- Writing an engaging headline is crucial for attracting readers.

9. Interview

Synonyms: Conversation, Dialogue, Discussion

Definition: A formal or structured conversation between an interviewer and interviewee, typically to gather information or elicit opinions.

Examples:

- The journalist conducted an interview with the author of the bestselling book.

- The job applicant prepared for the interview by researching the company.

- The interview revealed valuable insights into the subject's life and work.

10. Podcast

Synonyms: Audio program, Broadcast, Show

Definition: A digital audio or video series that can be downloaded or streamed, covering various topics and

often featuring discussions or interviews.

Examples:

- I enjoy listening to podcasts during my daily commute.

- The podcast hosts invited a renowned expert to discuss the latest trends.

- The podcast gained a large following due to its engaging content.

11. Audience

Synonyms: Viewers, Listeners, Readers

Definition: The group of people who receive or consume media content.

Examples:

- The television show attracted a wide audience of all age groups.

- The author's book appealed to a niche audience interested in historical fiction.

- The website's audience increased significantly after implementing SEO strategies.

12. Social media

Synonyms: Online networking, Digital platforms, Social networking

Definition: Internet-based platforms and applications that enable users to create, share, and interact with content and connect with others.

Examples:

- She spends a significant amount of time on social media, connecting with friends and sharing updates.

- The company used social media to launch its new product and engage with customers.

- Social media platforms have revolutionized communication and information sharing.

13. Blog

Synonyms: Weblog, Online journal, Diary

Definition: A regularly updated website or online platform where an individual or group shares personal experiences, opinions, or information.

Examples:

- She started a blog to document her travels and share travel tips.

- The fashion blog features articles on the latest trends and style advice.

- The blog post received numerous comments and sparked a lively discussion.

14. Media literacy

Synonyms: Information literacy, Digital literacy, Critical thinking

Definition: The ability to access, analyze, evaluate, and understand media messages and information critically.

Examples:

- Media literacy skills are essential in navigating the vast amount of information available online.

- Schools should prioritize teaching media literacy to empower students in the digital age.

- Media literacy enables individuals to differentiate between credible and misleading sources.

15. Documentary

Synonyms: Nonfiction film, Factual film, Real-life portrayal

Definition: A film or video presenting factual information, real events, or actual people, often with the intent to educate or raise awareness.

Examples:

- The documentary explores the impact of climate change on vulnerable communities.

- She watched a documentary about the history of space exploration.

- The documentary received critical acclaim for its powerful storytelling.

16. Journal

Synonyms: Diary, Log, Record

Definition: A written record or chronicle of personal experiences, thoughts, or observations.

Examples:

- She kept a journal to reflect on her daily activities and emotions.

- The scientist recorded the experiment's progress in his research journal.

- Writing in a journal can be a therapeutic practice.

17. Newsfeed

Synonyms: Timeline, Stream, Updates

Definition: A continuously updated list or display of news, posts, or content, usually on social media platforms.

Examples:

- He scrolled through his social media newsfeed to stay updated on current events.

- The newsfeed showed recent posts from friends and followed accounts.

- The algorithm curates the newsfeed based on the user's preferences.

18. Caption

Synonyms: Title, Description, Subtitle

Definition: A brief description or text accompanying an image, illustration, or video.

Examples:

- She wrote a witty caption for the Instagram photo she posted.

- The caption provided additional context for the photograph.

- The documentary included captions to aid understanding for viewers with hearing impairments.

19. Editorialize

Synonyms: Express an opinion, Interpret, Commentate

Definition: To express personal opinions or biases in presenting news or information, especially in journalism or writing.

Examples:

- The journalist was criticized for editorializing the news article instead of presenting facts objectively.

- The author's article editorialized the political situation, influencing readers' opinions.

- It's important for journalists to separate reporting from editorializing.

20. Media outlet

Synonyms: News organization, Publishing company, Broadcasting network

Definition: A company or organization that produces and disseminates media content, such as news, articles, broadcasts, or publications.

Examples:

- The newspaper is a respected media outlet known for its investigative journalism.

- The media outlet covered the breaking news story extensively.

- The online media outlet gained popularity due to its unique content.

25. Economics

1. Inflation

   Synonyms: Price increase, Rising prices, Cost of living

   Definition: A sustained increase in the general price level of goods and services in an economy over time.

   Examples:

   - Inflation can erode the purchasing power of consumers.

   - The government implemented measures to control inflation and stabilize the economy.

   - High inflation rates can negatively impact the economy and reduce consumer confidence.

2. Recession

   Synonyms: Economic downturn, Slump, Decline

   Definition: A significant decline in economic activity characterized by a contraction in GDP, increased unemployment, and reduced production and consumption.

   Examples:

   - The country experienced a severe recession following the financial crisis.

   - Businesses often struggle to survive during a recession.

   - The government implemented stimulus measures to revive the economy during the recession.

3. GDP (Gross Domestic Product)

   Synonyms: Economic output, National income, Production

   Definition: The total value of all goods and services produced within a country during a specific period, often used as a measure of economic growth.

   Examples:

   - The government aims to increase GDP by promoting investment and innovation.

   - The GDP growth rate is an important indicator of a country's economic health.

   - The country's GDP has been steadily increasing over the past decade.

4. Supply and demand
Synonyms: Market forces, Buying and selling, Commerce
Definition: The relationship between the availability of goods or services (supply) and the desire or willingness to buy them (demand) in a market.
Examples:
- The price of a product is determined by the interaction of supply and demand.
- When demand exceeds supply, prices tend to rise.
- Understanding supply and demand dynamics is crucial for successful business operations.

5. Unemployment
Synonyms: Joblessness, Unemployment rate, Worklessness
Definition: The state of being without a job, typically measured as a percentage of the labor force actively seeking employment.
Examples:
- The government introduced programs to reduce unemployment and create job opportunities.
- High unemployment rates can have social and economic consequences.
- He has been actively searching for a job but hasn't found employment yet.

6. Trade
Synonyms: Commerce, Exchange, Business
Definition: The buying and selling of goods and services between countries or regions.
Examples:
- International trade plays a vital role in the global economy.
- The government negotiated a trade agreement to facilitate exports and imports.
- The company expanded its operations to increase trade with foreign markets.

7. Investment

Synonyms: Capital expenditure, Financial commitment, Funding

Definition: The allocation of money or resources with the expectation of generating future income or profit.

Examples:

- Investing in stocks can provide long-term financial growth.
- The government encourages investment in renewable energy technologies.
- The company plans to allocate a significant portion of its budget to research and development.

8. Market

Synonyms: Marketplace, Exchange, Trading center

Definition: The mechanism or environment where buyers and sellers interact to facilitate the exchange of goods or services.

Examples:

- The stock market experienced a significant downturn.
- The company conducted market research to understand consumer preferences.
- The real estate market has been booming in recent years.

9. Entrepreneur

Synonyms: Business owner, Innovator, Founder

Definition: An individual who starts and operates a business, assuming financial risks in the hope of making a profit.

Examples:

- She is a successful entrepreneur who founded multiple startups.
- The government supports and encourages young entrepreneurs to foster innovation.
- Becoming an entrepreneur requires determination and a strong business acumen.

10. Fiscal policy

Synonyms: Government spending, Budgetary policy,

Economic policy
Definition: The use of government spending and taxation to influence and stabilize the economy.
Examples:
- The government implemented expansionary fiscal policies to stimulate economic growth.
- Fiscal policy aims to maintain a balanced budget and manage public finances.
- The finance minister announced new measures as part of the fiscal policy strategy.

11. Monetary policy
Synonyms: Central bank policy, Interest rate policy, Money management
Definition: The control of money supply, interest rates, and credit conditions by a central bank to achieve economic objectives.
Examples:
- The central bank adjusted interest rates as part of its monetary policy response.
- Monetary policy decisions can impact borrowing costs and consumer spending.
- The government closely monitors the effectiveness of monetary policy measures.

12. Tariff
Synonyms: Import duty, Customs tax, Trade barrier
Definition: A tax or duty imposed on imported goods, designed to protect domestic industries or generate revenue.
Examples:
- The government imposed tariffs on imported steel to support local producers.
- Tariffs can increase the price of imported products and affect consumer choices.
- The company faced challenges due to the new tariff regulations.

13. Deficit

Synonyms: Shortfall, Debt, Negative balance

Definition: The amount by which expenses or losses exceed income or revenue, often resulting in a negative balance or debt.

Examples:

- The country's budget deficit has increased significantly in recent years.

- The company needs to address its financial deficit to ensure sustainability.

- The deficit in the trade balance can impact a country's currency value.

14. Surplus

Synonyms: Excess, Overflow, Abundance

Definition: The amount by which income or revenue exceeds expenses or losses, resulting in a positive balance or excess.

Examples:

- The government announced a budget surplus, indicating a healthy economy.

- The surplus of goods in the market led to discounted prices.

- The company generated a surplus of revenue, allowing for further investments.

15. Subsidy

Synonyms: Grant, Financial assistance, Aid

Definition: Financial support or assistance provided by the government to individuals, businesses, or sectors to promote specific activities or achieve desired outcomes.

Examples:

- The government offers subsidies to encourage the adoption of renewable energy.

- Subsidies can help reduce the cost of essential services for low-income families.

- The company received a subsidy to develop innovative technologies.

16. Monopoly

Synonyms: Exclusive control, Domination, Hegemony

Definition: A market situation where a single company or entity has complete control over the supply of a particular product or service.

Examples:

- The company established a monopoly in the telecommunications industry.

- Monopolies can limit competition and potentially harm consumer interests.

- The government implemented regulations to prevent monopolistic practices.

17. Competition

Synonyms: Rivalry, Contest, Struggle

Definition: The activity or condition of competing against others, often in a market, with the aim of gaining an advantage, winning customers, or achieving success.

Examples:

- Healthy competition encourages innovation and improves product quality.

- The company faced intense competition from its competitors.

- The government promotes fair competition to ensure a level playing field.

18. Demand

Synonyms: Desire, Need, Requirement

Definition: The desire or willingness of consumers to purchase a particular product or service at a given price and time.

Examples:

- The company needs to analyze consumer demand to adjust production levels.

- The demand for organic food has increased in recent years.

- Changing consumer preferences can influence demand

patterns.

19. Supply

Synonyms: Provision, Stock, Availability

Definition: The total amount of a specific product or service that is available for purchase or consumption in the market.

Examples:

- The supply of raw materials is critical for manufacturing operations.

- The company ensures a steady supply of goods to meet customer demand.

- Supply chain management plays a crucial role in optimizing efficiency.

20. Exchange rate

Synonyms: Currency rate, Foreign exchange rate, Forex rate

Definition: The value at which one currency can be exchanged for another, determining the relative worth of different currencies in international trade and finance.

Examples:

- Fluctuations in the exchange rate can impact import and export costs.

- The company benefited from a favorable exchange rate when conducting business abroad.

- The central bank intervened to stabilize the exchange rate.

Manufactured by Amazon.ca
Acheson, AB

10957782R00120